The Wedding Mass

ARE YOU PLANNING A WEDDING?

Please note that inside the back cover of this book you'll find a pull-out section to indicate your preferences for the Wedding Ceremony.

You may simply pull-out the form, make your selections, and then present it to the priest or deacon who will be officiating at your wedding.

Reflections on the Road to Marriage
Wedding Mass Prayers and Readings
Wedding Ceremony Selections

LOVE, DATING, AND MARRIAGE

FATHER FRANK E. PAPA, S.O.L.T., J.C.D.

A Marriage Preparation Guide

Leaflet Missal Company
976 W. Minnehaha Ave.
St. Paul, MN 55104

Nihil Obstat: Rt. Rev. Msgr. Timothy J. Thorburn, JCL
Censor Librorum

Imprimatur: Most Reverend Fabian W. Bruskewitz, DD, STD
Bishop of Lincoln

April 26, 2004

The *Nihil Obstat* and *Imprimatur* are official declarations that a book or
a pamphlet is free from doctrinal or moral error. No Implication is
contained therein that those who have granted the *Nihil Obstat* and
Imprimatur agree with the contents, opinions or statements expressed.

Artwork

Virginia Broderick
Robert Laskey

Printed in U.S.A.

TABLE OF CONTENTS

Dedication
Foreword
Introduction

** Unless otherwise noted, all Biblical translations
are those of the author. **

Anatomy Of A Doomed Relationship
- The Downward Spin
- Illusion And Confusion
- Convinced But Confused
- "The Sense Of Guilt" Becomes Numbed
- Trouble Ahead
- What Went Wrong
- "Breaking-Up" Is Hard To Do

The Problem
- True Relationships And False Relationships
- Dating Too Young
- The Devil, Disaster, And Divorce
- Growing Their Separate Ways

The Question Of Intimacy
- How About Intimacy For Teens?
- Growing In Wisdom And Years
- A Flawed "Intimacy"
- Married Love Is Not A Teenage Thing
- Family Intimacy
- Treasured Moments

Married Love Is An Adult Thing
- Marriage Intimacy
- Married Love Is A Total Commitment
- Marriage: A Mature And Responsible Commitment

Marriage Is A Holy Thing
Reasonable And Responsible Dating

Marriage Is Not "Make Believe"
- "Getting Married"

Marriage: What Is It?
- Marriage Is An Unbreakable Contract
- Marriage Is A Permanent Relationship
- Marriage Is An Exclusive Relationship

Further Questions?
The Order Of The Mass For Marriage
The Wedding Mass Prayers

- Wedding Mass Prayers "A"
- Wedding Mass Prayers "B"
- Wedding Mass Prayers "C"

The Wedding Mass Readings

- Reading Selections From The Old Testament
- Reading Selections From The New Testament
- Responsorial Selections From The Psalms
- Alleluia Verses And Verses Before The Gospel
- Reading Selections From The Gospels

The Marriage Vows

- Consent To Marriage
- The Form Of Consent
    Form "A"
    Form "B"
    Alternative Form "A"
    Alternative Form "B"

The Blessing And Exchange Of Rings

- Blessing "A"
- Blessing "B"
- Blessing "C"

General Intercessions

- Prayer Of The Faithful "A"
- Prayer Of The Faithful "B"

Preface Prayers For Marriage

- Preface Selection I
- Preface Selection II
- Preface Selection III

AFTERWORD: LIFE AFTER THE WEDDING CAKE
- Prayer Of The Husband And Wife For Each Other
- Booklet Order Information
- "Pull-Out" Form: to indicate your preferences for choice of Wedding Mass Prayers; Wedding Readings; Form of Consent to Marriage; Blessing of Rings; Prayers of the Faithful; Preface Prayers. ("Wedding Preparation Checklist" is included).
- About the Author (Inside Back Cover)

DEDICATION

I wish to dedicate this book to a priest of God who was a spiritual father to me in my struggling youth, God's instrument in leading me to the Priesthood, and an inspiration to me now in my senior years. He is known affectionately as "Father Pat" to everyone around him; but I continue to this day to address him reverently as "Father Toscano" – even though we are now "brother" priests.

Father Pasquale Toscano never climbed high in ecclesiastical circles, he doesn't exhibit letters after his name, he has never been decorated with awards or titles; but for more than 60 years he has been a loyal priest devoted to Christ Jesus present in the Eucharist and to His Blessed Mother.

God love that cheerful priest.

Father Frank Papa, S. O. L. T.
August 22, 2003
Feast of Mary, Queen and Mother

FOREWORD

There is a plethora of books on love and marriage. Understandably it is a topic that interests everyone. Unfortunately, very many of these books, far from shedding light on the sacredness of marriage, offer a distorted picture of this great sacrament: either they water it down, or worse, they tell people what they want to hear. Isaiah was confronted with this unholy wish: "Prophesy not to us what is right: speak to us smooth things...." (*Isaiah* 30:10) R.S.V.-C.E. Aiming at financial success, authors of books on love and marriage tell young people that the meaning of life is self-fulfillment, that the teaching of the Church is too narrow, that they have a right to pursue happiness, and that they must liberate themselves from the taboos which have burdened the Catholic conscience for centuries.

Father Papa has understood the greatness and seriousness of marriage viewed in a Christian light. We live in a deeply troubled society. We no longer distinguish between necessities and luxuries. Who is more unhappy than a child who has everything and enjoys nothing. All our power and money have not succeeded in bringing us peace at home in the heart of the family. In our own society, marriage (and consequently the family) have broken down.

Father Papa, a veteran in the confessional, knows all the pitfalls into which many young people will tumble if they are not grounded in their faith: pitfalls such as booze, endless parties, wild music, drugs; anything which tears young people away from God. The traps are so numerous; but they have the same end: the loss of one's precious virginity. Once lost, the sin can be forgiven; but the virginity is lost forever.

The responsibility of educators is great: they are to inform young people of the beauty of love and marriage as instituted by God. May God have mercy on those who have failed to inform young people of all the dangers that threaten these treasures.

Father Papa's book aims at correcting this grave failure. Love is a great thing. But the word love is so abused in our society that young people confuse love with cheap romanticism and fleeting emotions – all redundant of soap operas. Love is not a superficial attraction of a handsome face or a well-built body. Love is a response to the beauty and nobility of a human being created in God's image and likeness. Love is steeped in reverence – not in superficial flashiness, good looks, sportive success, and the like. Such are not a sound basis for marriage.

Love is based on knowledge of another person – a knowledge of his relation to God, of his desire to follow God's commandments, a knowledge of whether he understands the depth and commitment required in marriage, a

10

test as to whether he grasps the mystery of intimacy and its link to procreation. To exclude God by artificial contraception is to exclude love: because God is love. Those who exclude God cannot procreate. They copulate – like animals, and the punishment is the sowing of the seeds of disunion: those couples who refuse to have children will most likely end in divorce – which is always an ugly affair. Moreover, it is costly.

Marriage has always been the linchpin of any healthy society. When radical permissiveness and the breakdown of marriage take over a society, it will suffer from a cancer which will soon destroy it. In such a society, young people are torn, unhappy, resentful, morally blind, irreverent, prone to "experiment" and prompted to escape from any responsibility. They are often tempted by suicide. "Freedom" proves to be slavery. They have no idea of the true meaning of life because they have not been told. Educators have failed to use their authority to **teach** and youth is their victim. The young have no idea of the beauty and sublimity of marriage and "have given up hope of reaching the heights" promised by the Church (cf. Dante's *Divine Comedy*", "Inferno", *Canto Primo,* 54).

Father Papa's book is an answer to a call. He gives us the teaching of the Church; he reminds us that love is not a craving for self-fulfillment, it is not a fleeting feeling divorced from our reason and our will. Love between a man and a woman finds its fulfillment and reveals its true beauty when it is sanctioned in the holy sacrament of matrimony, vitalized by grace. It is then a great source of happiness.

The Church has always understood that love is primarily procreative, and also unitive: love desires union. Even when a man and woman cannot have a progeny because of age or a quirk of nature, the Church still regards their marriage to be as much of a sacrament as those blessed by a large progeny. If their union is more spiritual and purer, it can glorify God more; but love must always be fruitful. A spiritual marriage with Christ can produce a great number of spiritual children. Mother Teresa of Calcutta had thousands and thousands of spiritual children.

Father Papa is offering a little book desperately needed: it gives us the teaching of the Church; and he had the felicitous idea of adding the beautiful Liturgy on marriage. Young people who are considering the noble state of marriage, should meditate carefully before taking this great step – which should lead them closer to God and to one another. Love is a great thing; so is marriage.

Dr. Alice von Hildebrand

INTRODUCTION

My dear friends,

When all is said and done, most men and women in this world get married.

When we consider the number of people in this world at any given time – only a select few enter the priesthood or religious life or remain single. Only a small percentage of men and women never marry. It's a good thing, because otherwise the human race would have gone out of existence a long time ago.

And if there were no married love between men and women, this would have been a far more chaotic world than it already is. In fact, most of the chaos of human history is due to the Fallen Nature of mankind, which usually expresses itself in the context of a dysfunctional married and family life! Destroy a marriage, and you destroy a family. Destroy families, and you destroy Society!

In our day, the sad thing is that about two out of every three marriages end up in a civil divorce a few years down the road. The bride and groom's wedding cake turns into ashes in their mouths.

What happened to the "love" that prompted them to marry each other? Were they *really* "in love"? During the "dating-period", were they *learning* to "love" each other, or were they *beginning* to "use" each other? Did they *really know* what they were doing?

When they entered into marriage, did they understand what they were consenting to? Could they have given a five-minute talk on the topic of Marriage? Were they aware of the rights and duties of their marriage? Could they have answered these and many other questions about something so serious as a "lifetime commitment" to marriage?

In this book, I'll try to treat these and other important questions about the awesome facts of Love, Dating, and Marriage. I hope to do so in a clear and concise way, because I know how busy young people are, as they strive to determine their life's mission and establish themselves in society!

And since you have perhaps obtained this book because you plan to have a wedding one of these days (maybe in the near future!), I've included a chapter devoted to the wedding ceremony itself. It has a special "pull-out" section, so that you may indicate to your parish priest your personal preferences, requests, and hopes concerning your wedding ceremony.

Every time I offer the Holy Sacrifice of the Mass, I will ask the good Lord to let His face shed its light upon any person who reads this book, that they may enjoy true love…here on earth and forever in Heaven.

Your friend,

Father Frank Papa, S.O.L.T., J.C.D.
c/o St. Mary's Church
15 Maplewood Avenue
East Hartford, CT 06108

CHAPTER I
LOVE

THAT MYSTERIOUS WORD

There is perhaps no word – in any language – that is more frequently used than the word: "Love."

"Love" is the main topic for songs, stories, movies, TV shows, poems, sayings, conversations, slogans, mottoes, debates, discussions, advertisements, billboards, letters, postage stamps, graffiti – you name it!

Who has not heard expressions such as: "I *love* my car"; I *love* baseball"; I *love* boating"; I *love* popcorn"; etc., etc., etc.

But do we *really* "love" all these things?

Actually, we don't really "love" things: we *use* them! Seldom do we see a person hugging a pizza. And if we do, we don't tend to think of that person as being in "love."

My point is that we "love" *persons;* not *things!* We "use" things. We may even "*like*" things; but we don't *love* them! We may "like" our dog very much; we may "like" the car we *use* every day; we may "like" ice cream or cookies or a cool beverage; so we *use* them to give us pleasure; but we don't really "love" them. It's hard to *love* a side of beef!

◊ We "love" *persons*; we should not "use" *persons*.

◊ We "use" *things*; we should not "love" *things*.

LOVE: WHAT IS IT?

Defining "love" in human words is a challenge. Love is not something you can pick up by hand, chew with your teeth, measure with a ruler, or weigh on a scale. Love is not a *material* thing; it is, rather, a *spiritual* thing. Love is more *super*-natural than natural.

NATURAL LOVE AND SUPERNATURAL LOVE

The best pagans are capable of a *natural* love for their spouses, relatives, and friends – a love which is incomplete and imperfect, but noble and elevating to a degree.

But baptized followers of Christ are capable of a *supernatural* love – founded on faith – prompting the person to love God as He is, and to love others because God wills it. A person would not be capable of *supernatural* love without God's Grace.

The Primary Symbol of Love is
Christ's Sacred Heart - beating
for each one of us

GOD'S DEFINITION OF LOVE

Our good God gives us *His* definition of love:

Love does no wrong to a neighbor....
(Romans 13:10)

Love is patient; love is kind. Love is not jealous, it is not boastful; it is not arrogant or rude. Love does not insist on its own way; it is not inclined toward anger; neither does it brood over injuries. Love does not rejoice in what is wrong, but rejoices in what is right. Love bears all things, is limitless in its trust, its hope, and its endurance of all things. Love is never-ending....
(1 Corinthians 13:4-8)

In other words, love takes some effort on our part.

LOVE REQUIRES SELF-SACRIFICE

God's definition of love obviously requires a willingness on our part to make *sacrifices* for the benefit of the person we love: it takes some *self-sacrifice* to be kind *always*, *never* to be jealous, boastful, arrogant, or rude to the person we love. It takes *self-control* not to insist on our own way, not to be inclined to anger, not to brood over injuries, etc.

A person who is unwilling to make sacrifices for you does not love you. The same is true if you are not willing to make sacrifices for him/her.

God says in Sacred Scripture:

"Love is a fire no waters avail to quench, no floods to drown; for love a man will give up all that he has in the world, and think nothing of his loss." *(Song of Songs 8:7)*

In fact, our Lord goes so far as to elevate Love to the level of a *supreme* sacrifice: He says:

"There is no greater love than this: that a man lay down his life for his friends." (John 15:13)

Anyone who would sacrifice his/her *own life* for another person has true love for that person. True love is spiritual, supernatural, and calls for self-sacrifice and self-control in our relationship to the one we love.

LOVE IS NEVER-ENDING

And: "Love is never-ending...."

A person who would say: "I don't love you any more," never loved you in the first place.

Love is a fire

no waters avail

to quench

no floods

to drown

Psalm 128:3

WHAT LOVE IS NOT

It might be useful to consider what love is *not*.

For instance:

- **Love Is Not A "Feeling"**

Love is not merely an *emotional* thing: Just because we "feel" good in the presence of another person, just because we experience "romantic feelings", just because we "feel" like we are in love, does not mean that we "are" in love. "Feelings" come and go. Our emotions go up and down; they never stay the same from one moment to another.

For example:

Consider a husband alarmed by his clock at 4:30 in the morning.

He sits on the edge of the bed and looks out the window into the darkness. Strong winds and icy sleet and deep-drifting snow cover his very long driveway which ends where unplowed streets begin.

As he tries to shake the sleep from his head, he finds himself dreading the long and difficult ride to his workplace, the tedious and stressful day at his job, and the bumper-to-bumper journey back home as the sun goes down.

He turns to look at his sleeping wife, adorned with hair curlers and a mud pack ("facial") on her face. It is safe to assume that – at that moment – he is *not* experiencing any *sentimental*, *emotional*, "feelings of love"! He does love his wife and his children; he is dedicated to making sacrifices for them; and he has willingly committed his whole life to them…but he is *not* – at this moment – enjoying "feelings" of love!

Likewise, when the wife remains at home in the role of "mommy" – her hair up in curlers, dressed down, cooking, cleaning, laundering, an infant in one arm, a soup ladle in the other hand, a second child around her neck, another at the apron strings, and still another grasping one of her ankles, and another dragging on the other leg, as she stirs the pot on the stove, and listens to Kevin reciting the times-tables – that wife and mother may not at that moment be enjoying sentimental, emotional "feelings of love"! Her love for her husband and children is *Spiritual*, *Supernatural*, *Sacrificial*! Her love is a matter of *the will*, not of emotion.

From time to time a person who is "in love" may experience "feelings" of love…but those "feelings" are *not* love! Sometimes, love may produce emotion; but emotion does not produce love.

Most of us – at one time or another – experience "feelings" that are noble and objective, not blinded by ill-founded emotions – emotions which are fully valid, sublime, and in full harmony with reasonable thinking and righteous intentions: feelings of compassion, feelings of mercy, feelings of contrition, etc. However, no sound relationship can be built on feelings. It would be a gross mistake to marry a drunkard or a drug-abuser because you are experiencing "feelings" of compassion – or "feelings" of mercy – or even "feelings" of love – toward the abuser!

Again:

Real love is not mere emotional, sentimental "feelings"; love is not an act of our nervous system. Rather, love is an act of our *intellect* and our *will*; we don't "fall" in love, we *choose* to love. Love is Spiritual, Supernatural, Sacrificial.

Furthermore,

- **Love Is Not "Sex"**

Love is not spelled "S-E-X". Love is not a sexual/sensual thing. Love is not a physical thing.

A man may be attracted by the *physical* appearance of a woman (or vice-versa), but this does *not* mean that he is "in love". The attraction is more for the *body* than for the *person*!

It would *not* be wise to marry someone for "looks" rather than for "love"! Our physical appearance changes with time. "Sex-appeal" does not last. Every minute we are alive, we are getting older. At 13 years old, we look quite different than we did when we were six years old. Over the years, our appearance changes radically! You need only look at your parents' wedding picture to see how they have changed in the span of your lifetime. As we advance in years, our face falls all over the place, we gain weight, or develop wrinkles, or lose hair, or drop a tooth or two; and then our "good looks" don't look so good!

"Love" endures. "Looks" do not! The "good looks" that attract you *today* will not be there *tomorrow*! When all is said and done, a guy could look like yesterday's lunch, and a girl could look like an old pair of boots, but if they are in True Love, she thinks, "He's so handsome!"; he thinks, "She's so beautiful!"

To sum up:

√ **"Feelings":** may be experienced from time to time during courtship and marriage; but it is not love! A "romantic" feeling is more "emotional" than "physical"; but it is *not* love!

√ **Sexuality/Sensuality:** too, is experienced at various times in a marriage. Sexuality is one *expression* of love, but it is *not* love itself. And while Sexuality is a magnificent "outward" expression of "inner" love, it is not the *only* "outward" expression of love: So, too are a hug, a kiss, holding hands, laughing together, smiling, joking, etc.; but even these physical expressions are **not** love itself.

√ **True Love:** "does *no wrong* to a neighbor." Unfortunately, sex can be an expression of *lust* rather than love. As we noted earlier, it is possible to *use* persons instead of loving them. If we *sin* in such a way, *using* our neighbor, or *leading* our neighbor into sin, we are not practicing love toward our neighbor. True love requires effort, self-control, and self-sacrifice for the one we love.

WHOM ARE WE SUPPOSED TO LOVE?

Christ Jesus our Lord teaches us:

*You shall **love the Lord your God** with all your heart,*
and with all your soul, and with all your mind.
*This is the great and **first** commandment. And*
*a **second** is like it, you shall **love your neighbor** as yourself.*

(emphasis added)
(Matthew 22:37-39 RSV/CE)

So: Our Lord makes it clear that we are to

- **Love God Above All,**

and

- **Love Our Neighbor** – (those *persons* He has placed in our lives).

SOME TYPES OF REAL LOVE

There are various types/kinds of love among persons:

√ Motherly Love
√ Fatherly Love
√ Brotherly/Sisterly Love
√ Friendly Love
√ Love for All Mankind
√ Married Love
√ etc., etc., etc.

In this brief book, we will focus on "Married Love".

In order to love someone as a friend, we must first get to know that person. And if we intend to commit the whole of our life to a husband or wife in that most intimate of friendships called "Marriage," it is *critically necessary* to "get to know" that person. For that reason, a man and woman spend a year or so, "courting" each other. In other words, they "date" each other on a *steady* basis. Which brings us to Chapter Two....

DATING

CHAPTER III
DATING

GOING ON "A" DATE

If you were to look-up the word "dating" in the Dictionary, you would find a variety of definitions. So I will explain how I'm using the word "dating" here.

By "dating", I mean a particular occasion when a man and a woman take part in a social activity together. That social activity might be bowling, or golfing, or tennis, or dining-out, or ice-skating, skiing, etc. It's a one-time event, but with an eye to further dates together, to get to know each other better.

There's only *one* purpose for "dating" at all: for the purpose of finding someone to marry. If a person is not prepared to get married, there's no reason to be "dating".

"STEADY"-DATING

"Steady"-dating would be a *number* of "dates" with the same person. These repeated, continuous, even *daily* "dates" would take place for the purpose of establishing a relationship that could lead to engagement and marriage within a year…or a year and a half (at the most). "Steady"-dating is also called "courtship".

Now, "dating" – "Going on a single date" – is one thing. It may turn out to be the one and only time they decide to date each other.

"Steady-dating" ("courtship") is *another* thing altogether! It will lead to a more involved relationship between the two persons. And if the steady-dating period extends beyond a year or so, it can lead to trouble, as we will see later.

ADULT STEADY-DATING

It is understandable that a man could go on a "date" with one woman this week and another one the following week; and still a third or fourth woman in later weeks – until he finds one that he may possibly be willing to spend the rest of his life with, in marriage. After dating her a few times, he may decide to date her *steadily*, in order to get to know her better, with an eye to making a decision to marry her in the not-too-distant future. (If he doesn't propose marriage to her within a year and a half, she should drop him like a hot potato. Things could drag-on for years, and he'll *never* marry her. We must beware of the person who keeps promising marriage, but never delivers on the promise!)

"Getting to know you"

- **Getting Involved Physically Or Emotionally**

Again, Dating is for those who intend to marry in the *near future*...within a year or so. Why? Because it is certain that a man and woman who progress to a second date, and then a third and fourth, and so on, will experience a rising degree of emotions toward each other, even though they may *not* actually be in love. They must take care **not** to allow themselves to become deeply involved *emotionally*; otherwise they will be tempted to use each other *sexually*. As we noted earlier, emotion and lust are not love. The couple must therefore be careful to *avoid intimate* physical contact during the courtship period. They must take care **not** to seek to be secluded from others, to be "away from the crowd."

These two adults – who are considering marriage – are presumed to be *friends*, to say the least. So they should behave as *friends* do. They should get together with *other* friends. They should meet in public. They may also take part in volunteer work; attend sporting events; take classes in art, sculpture, music; they may join a bowling team, tennis tournament, choir, band, or orchestra; go out to dinner with friends, etc. All such activities *lessen* the occasions for deep *emotional* entanglement or *sexual* temptation before marriage.

Nightclubs, bars, taverns, dance-halls, and the like, are not choice locations for finding someone you would like to marry.

REVIEWING AND EVALUATING OUR TEEN YEARS

No one reaches adulthood without first working through the years of adolescence. The teen years are an important period of our life – a time when we strive to grow "in wisdom...and in favor with God and man." (*Luke 2:52*) R.S.V.-C.E.

- **Mistaken Ideas**

But it often happens during these teen years that a person may acquire some mistaken notions about life and love. The result may be that a young man or woman will step into his/her adult years burdened by a limited understanding of life, love, and marriage.

So it might be useful to *review* and *evaluate* our teen years to see whether we've picked up some wrong ideas or faulty viewpoints about love, dating, and marriage along the way.

- **Teens And Dating**

What about "dating" for those who are in their teen years? The Worldlings say:

◊ "You don't have a boyfriend yet?"

◊ "You're already 9-10-11, and you haven't had a date yet?"

◊ "You really should be dating someone by now, shouldn't you?"

Actors, singers, magazines, newspapers, videos, TV commercials, Internet – you name it – are all promoting teen dating (and making heaps of money doing so). Many merchandisers do the same in their advertisements, asserting:

"Boys! Wear this 'fragrance' and the girls will be chasing you all over the place."
"Girls! Wear this perfume and the boys will knock down big trees and buildings to get to your door!"

● **Clothing And Cosmetics**

The clothing industry, for example, gains mountains of money by promoting "designer clothing" for teenagers – promising that, "It will make you look '*sexy*'!" (while it makes them grow "*rich!*")

Television portrays pre-teens (10-11-12 year olds), dressed like "ladies of the evening", or wearing "tops" that don't meet "bottoms", and "bottoms" that don't meet "tops"; nose-rings, tongue rings, eyebrow rings – and various other bizarre rings, (some of them worn specifically to signal sexual "preferences"); bathing suits that are similar in style to birthday suits (remember the "suit" you wore on the day of your birth?). Today there does not seem to be much *cloth* in the clothing industry! The *less* cloth they sell you, the *more* money they charge you. We pay more for less.

Some girls are pressured to wear so much make-up that if you bumped into them, their face would fall off. One guy tried to step on a spider approaching his girlfriend, and it turned out to be one of her false eye-lashes.

● **For Guys, Too!**

Some years ago the cosmetic and fashion industries decided they could double their money by tapping-into the egos of *males* as well as females. If they could profit by promoting the vanity of *females* – why not *males*, too?

Out came a line of "unisex" products: fragrances, jewelry, clothing (or lack of clothing) for men and women alike. The girls looked like boys; and the boys looked like girls. Sometimes it was hard to tell if you were walking behind "Eddie" or "Betty".

To put it briefly, the Worldlings (who wish to justify *their* own sexual misbehavior) – and the Profiteers (who wish to fill their pockets with *our* money) – are doing whatever they can to promote teen dating. It's in the air we breathe!

- **Love Is Not About "Looks" Or "Feelings"**

So, many young people are led to believe that "dating" is the thing to do. To speak *against* "dating" is a "hard sell". A guy and girl who have been dating steadily may *feel* sincere and passionate about their relationship. They are not aware that what they are "feeling" is not love, since love is not a *feeling*; nor is it a *physical* attraction. Love is an act of the *intellect* and the *will*.

- **"Safe-Sex" Before Marriage?**

To make matters worse, if they are *physically* involved, (especially with someone who has "had sex" with one or another individual) there is a strong possibility of being infected with a Sexually Transmitted Disease (STD) for which there is no cure. The guy and girl may be under the *illusion* (promoted by so-called "sex-experts") that they can practice **"safe-sex"** (which is anything but "safe"). They hope that by using condoms, plugs, or drugs, they will "protect" themselves from being infected with an STD; and prevent a pregnancy as well. But just reading the warnings on the package (in small or obscure print) is enough to alarm anyone but the "experts". These methods are unquestionably dangerous. **"Safe-sex *Guaranteed!*"** – you won't find *that* claim on the package!

- **Probability Of Pregnancy**

There is also the immediate or eventual probability of a pregnancy (Many babies are conceived on first dates!), followed by the temptation to murder their baby (while still in the-womb) by abortion. This does not create the best conditions for a loving marriage down the road.

The use of assorted "devices," in a risky, roulette-like attempt to prevent pregnancy, tends to leave something lacking in their "love," "spontaneity," and "sincerity". They busy themselves preparing for what they think will be..."protected sex"...and they find that it takes-away from their "spontaneity-in-love". Such devices do *nothing* for True Love; nor do they guarantee "disease-free" or "pregnancy-free" sex. The guy and girl find the devices awkward and embarrassing; and after trying it one time, they never again bother with it. They end-up telling themselves: "This is nonsense!" (and they're right!)..."I'm not doing this!" And they don't. They let the so-called "professionals" use the foolish devices! The guy says: "Hey...we're in love! If you get pregnant, I'll be responsible." But when a pregnancy takes place, he's severely tempted to say: "Well! What do you *mean*, 'Let's get married'? I'm not going to *ruin* my life just because *you* got pregnant!...And by the way, what do you mean: *I'm* the father?"

And there goes their false idea of "love" right out the window. Reality rushes in like a harsh wind.

ANATOMY OF A DOOMED RELATIONSHIP

It all begins so innocently. The Devil gets you by degree…little by little:

The boy and girl meet each other at a party.

They may be attracted to each other because "she's beautiful" or "he's so handsome". Or, they may be attracted to each other because they "feel" good when they are in each other's presence. Their attraction, then, has to do more with *physical* appearance; or *emotional* "feelings". It isn't love…but nevertheless that's what they innocently think it is.

Their relationship begins with simple conversation. After a couple of "dates", they hold hands together in the presence of their parents. Later they seek to have conversations *away* from the presence of others. Then, one will say to the other: "You know, I love you." And the other will respond: "Yeah?…Well, I love you, too."

- **The Downward Spin**

They begin to steady-date. When the boy and girl are separated from each other – even for a day – they experience a sense of "need" to be together, to speak with each-other face to face; or at least by some modern means of communication. They enjoy talking to each other for as long as they can, about anything at all… the day's events, their studies… or their "feelings" about one another.

They look forward to those times when they can be together – at a school dance, sporting event, or whatever; then they're able to spend time with this person whom they believe they "love". They "feel" *very happy* to be with that person – holding hands at first. At this point, there may not yet be sexual intercourse…not that one or the other doesn't *think* about it (at least on the part of the guy…Yeah…he thinks about it!).

Then they seek to be alone together; and when that starts happening, they don't just hold hands. Now there's hugging; and then long embraces; then it's kissing; which develops into passionate caressing; and that, of course, leads to sexual intercourse!

- **Illusion And Confusion**

The boy and the girl are under the illusion that they will *never* be dating anyone else, other than *this one* whom they believe they love. They suppose that they are being "exclusive" to each other.

Their desire for intimacy – which started off so innocently by just holding hands (which the boy and girl saw as "nothing wrong") – inevitably develops into what appears to be an "exclusive" relationship. From there it moves on to that "kissing stage" mentioned earlier; which progresses toward passionate kisses and caresses; which degenerates into sexual intercourse *outside* marriage; which threatens a probable pregnancy, followed by the temptation to murder-by-abortion the child they will have "accidentally" conceived.

- **Convinced But Confused**

Their sexual relationship proceeds on the assumption that – on some *vague* day in the future – "This relationship will lead me to marry my high school sweetheart." Their physical intercourse *seems* to "bond" them together, generating a sense of being *even closer* to each other. The boy and the girl become *more convinced* than ever, that they "love" each other, and – after high school "We'll get jobs and get married."

Whether they are teenagers or adults, persons are *confused* if they think that sex is love. They may truly believe that they are "in love"; but regrettably, time will prove them sadly wrong. While love can beget sex, sex does not beget love.

- **"The Sense Of Guilt" Becomes Numbed**

Once things have developed to this stage, any sense of guilt that they may have experienced earlier is gone. Any awareness they may have had previously, that they were sinning gravely against God, is clouded over by their impulses. Any knowledge they had that Society would say, "This is wrong; you're not supposed to do that until you're married," is ignored. Their sense of guilt is gone. All that remains are the "feelings", the physical "attraction", the sexual passion. The baser instincts take over. Their "intimate" relationship is kept a *secret* shared only by the two of them. No one else is aware of it except them alone. There's something delicious about the secrecy. They continue to profess a "love" for each other; but it is a "love" fueled by *emotion* and *sex*, and a misconception that they are being "adult".

- **Trouble Ahead**

But underneath it all, a troublesome *thought* keeps surfacing from time to time:

> "This is all wrong. People know that this is unacceptable. Sex is not something you're supposed to do until you're *married*. But here we are, *doing* it. Those who say, 'It's OK', *know* it isn't; they say that alcohol and drug abuse is 'all right', too, but they're just trying to excuse-away what they're doing."

As time passes, they both begin to experience problems in their relationship. They've been enjoying the *emotional* and *physical* pleasures they've gotten from each other; but their encounters do not have a spiritual/sacrificial side; there's no true *bond* there. They begin to sense that what they have been doing was a mistake.

Their "intimacy", their "exclusive" *attachment* to each other falls away. After a while, they're just not satisfied or willing to continue with this "exclusive dating" arrangement; but they continue seeing each other *anyway* because they don't want to hurt the other party. But eventually they get past that problem, too. They get to the point where one party orchestrates a *conflict*, so that they can "break-up". He/she finds "reasons" to *end* the relationship. They argue. The planned "future" marriage between the two "high school sweethearts" *dies* before it is born. In a way, it is a blessing. More tragic are those teenage marriages which *do* take place, and then die *after* they are born!

- **What Went Wrong**

The trap was set by the Devil; and they both walked into it. He brought them along step by step; but the steps led downward. The couple thought they were climbing the heights of love, while instead their *relationship* was on the downhill road to ruin; it's not going to last. Their initial excitement and sexual "intimacy" will eventually become common; they'll get used to it; the exhilaration will be gone; and that will translate in their minds as: "The love is gone. There is no sense in continuing this relationship since we no longer find each other emotionally exciting or sexually attractive."

- **"Breaking-Up" Is Hard To Do**

And once they get *bored* with the sex – and the emotions are *not there* anymore – the relationship dies. Their relationship is over except for the shouting. The two parties have become very accustomed to each other, and that *excitement* of "having sex" together is no longer there. The thrill of the relationship is gone.

Then they "feel" that they have fallen out of love, and their relationship begins to deteriorate. If, say, the guy decides to "break-up" the relationship before the girl does (or vice-versa), the party on the "receiving-end" of the deal feels very hurt, and may feel rejected for any number of reasons:

"I'm not appealing any more."
"He's found somebody else."
"She's found another guy."

THE PROBLEM

The problem is that they have confused their "*sex*" with love. They have confused their "*feelings*" as love. They didn't realize that their "sex" was not going to remain *exciting*; it was bound to bring them to the conclusion that: "We're no longer in Love."

And in fact they were *not* in love; they were in "sex". The boy was not working to support the girl, to build a life together, to have children, to have a home. The girl was not involved in preparing to raise a family, to nurture her children, to keep house, to spend long years at the stove and table, under one roof, because of her love for her husband and her children.

They *weren't*, they *aren't*, and they very likely *never will be*..."married" to each other!

In some unfortunate cases, such young people *do* marry, usually because the girl "got pregnant." But then, throughout the years, a frequent and nagging question keeps surfacing in their minds:

"Did he marry me because he felt he *had* to? After all, I *was* pregnant!"

"Did she marry me because she *loved* me, or because she 'felt' she *needed* me because she was pregnant?"

This does not exhaust the list of possible doubts that will come to their minds over the years, nor does it exhaust the number of bitter arguments and disputes they will engage in over the years, due to those doubts.

- **True Relationships And False Relationships**

The difficulty is to make a clear distinction between a *true* intimate relationship and a *false* one: A *false* intimate relationship has all the *outward* signs of marriage, but none of the *inward* Grace: it "looks" like love, it "feels" like a marriage, but it's *not* love *or* marriage. A false relationship built on emotion or sex does not normally lead to a happy marriage. Instead, those false relationships end up in ashes...time and again.

Those who take part in such a relationship might object:

"How can you say we're *not* in love? We '*bond*'...we're '*exclusive*'...*our* relationship is '*permanent*,'...isn't it?"

But what they're *doing*, what they're *expressing*, what they're *feeling*, is *not* what they think it is. Emotional and sexual intimacy *outside* marriage is *not* to be confused with a life-time commitment to true married love.

- **Dating Too Young**

As we noted earlier, the Worldlings push teens to grow up too fast – to be adults – to wear the make-up, to use the products, to dress as adults. But, they are too young; they are teens. They're *not* adults yet! They're not at the point of adulthood. They would like to be; but they are not. They are being "robbed" of the time to enjoy being young – which "goes by" fast enough as it is. Some day they will look back at this period of their life and find that their youth was spent with nothing to show for it other than an "ex" boyfriend or girlfriend; and perhaps some real shame and sorrow for the behavior they engaged in...some real shame and heart-ache (There's no getting away from that!). They may also cause grave hurt to their parents and other family members. And if they become involved in such *immoral* behavior, God is not pleased, either.

- **The Devil, Disaster, And Divorce**

The Devil pulls them down step-by-step, degree-by-degree, and sets them on a foundation that crumbles. The boy and girl are neither mature enough, nor experienced enough, to undertake what true love is; they're not in a position to make a lifetime commitment; nor do they have the financial means, education, social skills, employment, etc., necessary to contract a marriage and raise a family. In effect, they are *playing* "house", they're *playing* "husband and wife". But, love and marriage are not "child's play"...or "teen's play," for that matter.

The things they are experiencing, the "feelings" they're indulging-in, give them a sense that: "Yeah, we're 'loving' each other; and we're being 'adult' about it." But what is taking place is exactly the *opposite*; they're *not* being "adult" about it; and the whole reason they're doing what they're doing is based on *errors* in their thinking. They're confused about the whole notion of love and marriage. If they *do* marry, it almost always ends in *divorce* down the road.

Again, the whole relationship may start out innocently. The boy and girl may be very sincere. They may really think that they are "in love", and they do intend to "get married" some day. But that "day" may take years to arrive! They've still got to get through high school and maybe college. Then they'll have to seek a career or find employment.

- **Growing Their Separate Ways**

And other factors enter the equation: Over the course of their youthful relationship, both individuals are maturing and living and growing in different ways: They may go to different colleges or jobs; they may meet different people; they will have different life experiences; They develop different viewpoints and goals. They may drift apart physically and emotionally. The possibility that their relationship will deteriorate is *high*. The probability that their future marriage will be a success is *poor*.

THE QUESTION OF INTIMACY

- **How About Intimacy For Teens?**

At times, a young person may sense that the most important need of his/her life is to *love* and to *be loved*. He/she may experience a thirst for *affection* – a thirst that should be fulfilled at *home*, between the members of the family.

The family should be the school where we learn the first things about genuine love – about loving others and about *being loved* ourselves.

However, as we mentioned earlier, we should not only seek to *be* loved; we must also strive to love our neighbor in return. Our Lord directs us to love others *first*, even to the point of sacrificing our very *life* for them.

And even if we do *not* receive love from others, our Good God loves us; and He will reward us for loving our neighbors as He commands. "It is in giving that you receive." Whatever we do for others, we should put our whole heart into it, as if we were doing it for the Lord and not for men. (See *Colossians 3:23*.)

- **Growing In Wisdom And Years**

There are only seven years of teenage life. The seven years of teenage life prepare us for the fifty or sixty years of adult life. Our teenage years are a time of preparation for the adult years – a time to learn about personalities and human relationships. The *casual* relationships of adolescence prepare us for the *lasting* relationships of adulthood. During our teenage years, our minds develop, and we become more conscious of the world, and people, and events, and the realities of life – in and around us. We become more *practiced* and *experienced* in the "techniques" and "tools" of life and of relationships. Our successes and failures in dealing with various and assorted *persons* and *personalities* – their characters and temperaments – are important experiences. And it is most important to have the support and intimacy of family life at home to help us grow in "wisdom and in years and in favor with God and man." (See *Luke 2:52*.)

- **A Flawed "Intimacy"**

Sometimes, persons in their teenage years – for unfortunate reasons – drift away from family intimacy and mistakenly seek to establish a strong, firm relationship with a member of the opposite sex. As we noted earlier: at first, there may not be any *physical* intimacy; but they do want to "be together exclusively"; and to profess to each other that: "I love you." Eventually, these sentiments lead to thoughts that they will marry at some undetermined future date.

- **Married Love Is Not A Teenage Thing**

Though they "feel" that they are "in love" and are going to marry "someday", a teen relationship will likely *end* before their high school years are over. It will be *done*! The 1% who do marry after high school almost always suffer through a failed marriage; they don't graduate college, nor do they learn a trade; they often end-up with an unfulfilling career and money problems! The wages they earn while living at home with their family seems like a lot of money. But once they are married and *earning that same pay*, they will not be able to "make ends meet". They will become aware that their parents had to **buy** the house they were living in; and they had to **pay** for the food and clothes and car and insurances and taxes necessary to marry and have a family.

The young couples' false "Love" *blinds* them to these realities. And other realities: They deprive themselves of the intimacy of the family – the special things done together as a family. They rebel against family activities because they want to be with their boyfriend or girlfriend. And if their parents "give-in", the teens lose the opportunity to interact as a loving family and thereby miss what family life *is*! Their "steady-dating" causes them to lose the enjoyment of "family".

- **Family Intimacy**

There is normally a good measure of warm intimacy between members of a family: Parents kiss their children. Children kiss their parents (and sometimes the family pet!). A son kisses his mother. A daughter kisses her father. A toddler kisses her infant brother. Grandparents kiss their grandchildren, and grandchildren kiss their grandparents. It is not unusual to see a child sitting on his mommy's lap, or carried on his daddy's shoulders. Another child may cling to his daddy's leg as his father walks across the room. A dignified dad may be observed crawling on his hands and knees as his children ride on his back. Brothers play-wrestle with each other. Uncles and aunts and cousins exchange hugs and kisses at holiday gatherings. These are not unusual occurrences.

- **Treasured Moments**

Moments like these are often treasured for the whole of our lives. It is certainly appropriate and commendable that such signs of affection take place among family members and relatives. In later years, we may cherish the memory of these family intimacies. We cherish the memory of those who are dear to us: their presence among us, their size, or their strength, their sensitivity, their humor, their friendliness, their good character, their warmth, their charm, their personality. We may recall the "fun stuff" done together: jumping for joy when "Daddy" came home from work; going shopping with Mom; looking forward to visits from relatives at Christmas; going fishing with Grandpa at Cedar Lake; going to the ball park with Dad to watch a game; going out to lunch and shopping with Grandma; going for a ride in the country with the family, or on a camping trip, or a vacation tour, or a trip to the amusement park, or on a picnic, or the like.

Of course, it is the role of family members to watch out for each other, take care of each other, help each other, and support one another in times of need or distress; sharing the joys and triumphs, trials and tribulations of life. All such moments are part of the experience of family intimacy.

But there is another type of intimacy that is altogether different: **Marriage Intimacy** – the intimacy experienced by a husband and wife.

MARRIED LOVE IS AN ADULT THING

- **Marriage Intimacy**

The relationship between a husband and wife is so intimate that the two persons become as one, in an embrace that is capable of procreating new human beings – new human *life* – as the fruit of their love for each other.

It is all so different when such "bonding" takes place between a husband and a wife who are committed to each other for life – in an adult, loving marriage. Only *then* will a man and woman experience a *bliss* which is reserved for a husband and wife alone. No other humans in any other situation can experience that bliss. *Lust* is no substitute for *Love*. Only in a loving marriage can a husband and wife experience that *unique* emotional, physical, and spiritual intimacy which strengthens their union, builds a very strong bond between them, and brings the two individuals closer together, so that they both share in a truly *exclusive*, *unbreakable*, relationship. Their intimacy is such that he and she *alone* are united as husband and wife, in a partnership of their whole life.

Likewise, their intimacy as a married couple is directed toward their mutual *well-being*: their spiritual, social, emotional, physical, financial, etc., *well-being*.

- **Married Love Is A Total Commitment**

When a man and woman are devoted to each other in marriage, their love fuels the desire to be together as *one*, even physically. Their married love is a *total commitment* of their whole lives to each other, "to have and to hold,…for better, for worse, for richer, for poorer, in sickness and in health," until death parts them. (See "Rite of Marriage.") It is this willingness to make *self-sacrifice*, this *total giving* of one's self in mind and heart to the one you love, that prompts the husband and wife to share in the act of sex in marriage – which bonds them together more closely, more intimately – and assists them in solidifying their union of mind and heart.

Again, married love is giving yourself *totally* – mind, heart, and will – *not merely sexually* – to the one you love. This is a *commitment* most people in their teen years are not capable of making…or fulfilling.

- **Marriage: A Mature And Responsible Commitment**

In fact, there are many *adults* in our day who are not sufficiently prepared or informed or mature enough to: "get married".

There is a tremendous difference between a mature, totally committed relationship based on true love and self-sacrifice, and a false relationship built on sex and emotion. The *false* version is severely lacking because of what it is *based* on: *sex* and/or "*feelings*".

Adults who are misinformed, irresponsible or immature are poor examples of how to establish a loving relationship. Often, persons in their teen years imitate them, in the belief that they are going to share and enjoy the things that these "adults" do. The boy and girl may reason that: "*Adults* have this 'intimacy'; *we're* going to have it, too!" They overlook the fact that such "intimacy" often brings *new children* into the world; and the teen is in *no* position to raise and educate them.

MARRIAGE IS A HOLY THING

When a marriage takes place between a man and woman who are both *Baptized*, that marriage is raised to the dignity of a Sacrament by Christ the Lord Himself, giving the husband and wife a share in the Life of God Himself.

Their Sacramental marriage, then, becomes something holy, sacred, and solemn...that union of husband and wife is a living image of the intimate and unbreakable union of Christ with His Mystical Spouse the Church.

Through the *Sacrament* of Matrimony, Christ *assists* the married couple to live together in love until death; and helps them fulfill their loving responsibility to procreate and raise their children in the fear and love of God.

REASONABLE AND RESPONSIBLE DATING

In summary: If a person is not ready or prepared to marry, he/she is not in a position to start dating. There is no other godly reason for dating, than to find someone to marry.

When a person is in the market to get married, and he/she begins steady-dating someone with an eye toward marriage, the courtship should last no longer than a year and a half. By then, the Wedding Invitations should be in the mail.

To begin to date someone *without* the impending prospect of marriage opens the door to a "relationship" built on mere emotion and/or physical (sexual) attraction. Such "relationships" inevitably drift into the realm of disappointment, conflict, bitterness, sorrow, and shame. The aim of such a couple is to love; but their sights are off-target and seldom travel the distance. When a marriage does take place, it most often ends in divorce. (One of the smaller States in the U.S.A. recently granted more than 17,000 divorces in one year, leading to an awesome number of broken homes and troubled lives for spouses and their children.)

A man and a woman who begin to date each other in a reasonable and responsible way may find in each other the person they wish to marry. The spark of unselfish love which begins to grow in them each day of their courtship will prompt them to look forward to spending the rest of their life together in **Marriage**...which is the topic of our next chapter.

MARRIAGE

CHAPTER III
MARRIAGE

Whenever a main character in a TV series is portrayed as "getting married", the whole world tunes in. People like a wedding! Even a "make-believe" one.

Who has any idea of the number of speeches, novels, poems, movies, TV shows, comics, cartoons, soap-operas, magazine articles, newspaper stories, newscasts, etc., that have "Marriage" as a topic?

And yet, many of those who write, or speak, or sing, or portray marriages, or advise others about marriage, don't have the foggiest notion what *real* marriage is all about! The result is that they produce what turns out to be *real* "fantasy", rather than a *real* portrayal of marriage.

MARRIAGE IS NOT "MAKE-BELIEVE"

It's easy to recognize "fantasy" in a cartoon, when we see a duck "marrying" a squirrel. But it's *not* so easy to detect the "fantasies" about marriage when you're watching some handsome actor "marrying" a pretty actress in a TV soap-opera. It may *seem* more "real" to us. But in fact, they are merely acting-out a script, written by a team of writers who together don't have a clue as to what true marriage is all about. Put their ideas of marriage in the duck, and he'd fly upside-down; the squirrel would walk backwards. The scriptwriters themselves are often in a broken marriage; or involved in a child-custody battle; or charged with non-support; or entangled in divorce proceedings.

- **"Getting Married"**

One of the most important decisions a person will make in his/her life is to "get married". *Getting married* is serious business; it is not something to be taken lightly. A man and woman who are planning to marry should *know* what they're *doing* **before** they start dating! It's wise to *know* how to swim *before* jumping into the middle of an ocean! We would prefer to be a passenger in a plane with a pilot who *knows* how to fly *before* he takes the controls.

MARRIAGE: WHAT IS IT?

The term "Marriage" comes from the word "Matrimony". And the word "Matrimony" is derived from the Latin word **mater** which means *mother*; and, perhaps, **munis**, which means *duty*. "Matrimony" (Marriage), then, is about the *duty of motherhood*! And, of course, "motherhood" does not normally happen without "fatherhood"! (I am aware that there have been

"Mother And Child"

occasional, successful attempts to conceive babies in laboratories; but who wants a test tube for a father and a petri-dish for a mother?)

Furthermore, in order for a marriage to have a father and mother, you need a *man* and a *woman*! Not a man and a man! Not a woman and a woman! This may be obvious to you, but there are folks out there who haven't figured this out yet. Sacred Scripture tells us that God joined together Adam and Eve – a man and a woman – in marriage. Some people mistakenly think that God joined together "Adam and Steve"! But "Adam and Steve" can't *conceive*!…Neither can "Madam and Eve"!

- **Marriage Is An Unbreakable Contract**

Marriage is a sacred, unbreakable **contract** between a man and a woman. (The term *"covenant"* is sometimes used; they both mean the same thing.) By means of that *contract*, the man and woman establish a *partnership of their whole life*! The husband and wife solemnly *commit* themselves to *each other* (and *no one else*), for as long as they are both alive!

- **Marriage Is A Permanent Relationship**

The human spirit recognizes that marriage is a **permanent** commitment. Marriage is a most serious union, binding the man and woman together for life, in a relationship so close and intimate that it will influence the rest of their lives together. The exact nature of their future isn't known to them; but it will have its hopes and disappointments, successes and failures, pleasures and pains, joys and sorrows. So on the day of their wedding, the Bride and Groom don't know what lies ahead in their life together, yet they vow before God and man, to take each other in marriage, "for better or for worse, for richer or for poorer, in sickness and in health **till death do us part.**" The man and woman must have a firm faith in each other in order to be willing to make such a serious vow as that in the presence of God and man.

"…Till death do us part." Therefore, marriage between a man and a woman is *unbreakable*; it lasts for the whole of their lives. Marriage is for keeps! If one or both of them intend to "stay married" only for a while, they would *not* be "getting married" at all! The attempt to marry would be null. Marriage is not a *temporary* thing. No reasonable person would wish to be wedded to someone who intends to leave him/her after a while.

God complains in Sacred Scripture about those who divorce; He says to them:

> *And here is another thing you do: you cover*
> *the altar of the Lord with tears, with weeping and*
> *wailing, because He now refuses to regard the*
> *offering or to accept it from your hands. And you*

ask, 'Why?' It is because the Lord is a witness
between you and the wife of your youth, with
whom you have broken faith, though she is your
companion and your wife by covenant. Did not
God make a single being that has flesh and the
breath of life? And what does He desire from
this single being? God-given offspring. So be
careful for your own life, and do not break
faith with the wife of your youth. For I hate
divorce, says the Lord God of Israel, and I hate
those who wear their sins on their cloaks, says
the Lord of hosts. So safeguard your own life,
therefore, and do not break faith in this way.
(Malachi 2:13-16)

Even a little child looks at his father and mother and presumes that:
"*This* is my daddy; and *this* is my mommy: FOREVER."
"*This* is daddy's wife; and *this* is mommy's husband: FOREVER."
It is the same with adults. No matter what age we are, we would not be happy to hear of the divorce of our parents. We would rather have it that our parents would be together, *forever*; and that they would love each other, *forever*.
When some religious leaders tried to test Our Lord by asking Him:

"Is it lawful for a man to divorce his wife for any reason
whatever?" He said in reply, "Have you not read that at
the beginning the Creator 'made them male and female'
and declared, 'for this reason a man shall leave his father
and mother and cling to his wife, and the two shall become
one flesh'? Thus they are no longer two, but one flesh.
Therefore, what God has joined together, let no man
separate."
(Matthew 19:3-6)

Married love is for a lifetime!
Why?
◊   First and foremost: **to bring forth children** and to **educate** them
◊   Secondly: for the **well-being** of the husband and wife
As the saying goes; "I'll love you *forever*!" As we noted earlier: If a person says, "I don't love you *anymore*"…he/she never did!

What God has joined together
let no man separate

- **Marriage Is An Exclusive Relationship**

Marriage is between "him" and "her" *alone*. No other man or woman is to enter the picture. Married love does *not* include a third person.

For example: a groom cannot take a bride for his wife and at the same time intend to carry on a relationship with *another* woman. At the wedding, he would be *pretending* to consent to the marriage by saying "I *do*" – when in fact, he *really* means: "*I don't!*" He would *not* be "getting married" at all!...Marriage is an e*xclusive* relationship between *this* man and *this* woman; and no one else!

Even a child (who couldn't speak for one-minute on the topic of marriage) would react with horror and confusion if he were to witness his daddy or mommy "carrying-on" with some *stranger* in the house! Nor would the innocent husband or wife be delighted with such an arrangement either!

Humans instinctively *know* that marriage is an *exclusive* commitment between *one* man and *one* woman only.

As Our Lord proclaimed:

> *Everyone who divorces his wife and marries another commits adultery, and he who marries a woman divorced from her husband commits adultery.*
> *(Luke 16:18) R.S.V.-C.E.*
> *You shall not commit adultery.*
> *(Matthew 19:18) N.A.B.*

- **Marriage Is A Sacrificial Gift Of Yourself To The One You Love**

Their sacred Wedding Vow requires that the husband and wife be willing to offer themselves in *self-sacrifice* to each other in order to fulfill the solemn obligations of their marriage. Right from the first day of their marriage, the bride and groom will voluntarily give up their lives as individuals, for a deeper and wider life together in common. Only love can make their sacrifices *easy*. Perfect love can make their sacrifices a *joy*. Only to the degree that the husband and wife love each other, will they be willing to make the self-sacrifices necessary to preserve their married life together.

Perfect love incites complete sacrifice. Think of God's love for us: He loved the world so much that He *sacrificed* His only begotten Son; and the Son loved us so much that He *sacrificed Himself* for our salvation. (See *Roman Ritual*, 1964.) He taught us that there is no greater love than when a man *sacrifices his very life* for the one he loves. (See *John 15:13*.)

To sum it all up:

In married love a man and a woman offer their very selves to each other. They *sacrifice* their own wills and desires for the benefit of the person they love. They offer to each other the sacrificial gift of :

◊ A **Permanent** Commitment: *"Until Death Do Us Part"*

◊ An **Exclusive** Commitment: *No other man or woman* in the relationship

Two other wondrous Gifts between a husband and wife are:

◊ Their **Sexuality** (according to the demands of love)

◊ Their **Fertility** (their capability to produce new human life)

The love of a husband and wife should be directed towards a *unity* between them, a unity that is deeply personal, a unity that goes *beyond* their union in one flesh, a unity that leads them to become one in heart and soul. In order to accomplish this, the husband and wife must be totally faithful to each other. But their union must strive to go *beyond* their loving interchange and contrive to bring *new life* into this world: children – the fruit of their love – if God should will to grant them! (See Pope Paul VI, Encyclical Letter *Humanae Vitae* , 25 July 1968. Pope John Paul II has articulated and repeated these facts as well.)

THE REASONS FOR MARRIAGE: WHY GOD FOUNDED MARRIAGE

- **The Primary Reason For Marriage: The Procreation And Education Of Children**

In marriage, a man and woman share in a giving of their very *selves* – even their *fertility*. Nothing is held back. And oftentimes, this intimate union of husband and wife produces the wonderful fruit of their love: the procreation of a *living child*, the conception of a *new life*! A new human being, destined to be a citizen of Heaven, is brought into this world! The husband and wife fulfill God's command that couples who are joined in marriage should strive to: **"Be fruitful and multiply; fill the earth."** *(Genesis 1:28)* At their wedding, the bride and groom freely give and receive the gift of each other's bodies for the purpose of procreating children (if God should so bless them).

A person who does not intend to have children is not capable of contracting a marriage! To *exclude* children is to *exclude* marriage!

Raising children requires responsibility, dedication, and self-sacrifice on the part of the parents. In order to accomplish this they will need a good measure of God's *Grace/Help*, through the noble and holy Sacrament of Matrimony. It is through the Sacrament of Marriage that

"Be Fruitful And Multiply"

Christ acts to give the Baptized man and woman the special Grace/Help they need to fulfill their duties as father or mother to the children they bring into this world as the fruit of their love.

- **The Secondary Reason For Marriage: The Well-being Of The Husband And Wife**

God is the Founder of marriage: therefore marriage was holy since the beginning of the world. Now our Lord Jesus Christ has made marriage *even holier* by raising it to the dignity of a Sacrament…one of the great mysteries of our Holy Catholic Religion. When a man and a woman come to church to get married, they are about to be *united* in a most sacred and serious way. God gives the man and the woman a share in His greatest creative work: the continuing of the human race. Through the Sacrament of Matrimony, the husband and wife are enabled to help each other to live spiritually good lives, and to live together in harmony, under God's Fatherly care. Their loving, unbreakable marriage is a living, effective image of *Christ's own* loving and unbreakable marriage to His Mystical Bride: the Church. And of course, the husband and wife should model *their* marriage according to the example of Christ!

THE SACRED DIGNITY OF MARRIAGE

Our Lord Jesus Christ blessed and raised marriage from its *natural* state to a *supernatural* state: marriage is now something *sacred*. Marriage is so important in God's eyes, that He decided to *help* husbands and wives to live together in *happiness* and *holiness*!

- **The Sacrament Of Matrimony**

Through the Sacrament of Matrimony, Christ *Himself* acts in the marriage. He assists a husband and wife throughout the days and years of their married life!

Christ enters their married life and gives them enabling Grace to offer themselves to each other in true love. In fact, the greatest possessions of their married life will be their intimate love for each other, and the fruit of that love: their children.

THE MASS AND THE OTHER SACRAMENTS AS GOD-GIVEN HELPS THROUGHOUT YOUR MARRIED LIFE

In order to keep God within us always, we need His Saving Help: we need His Grace: we need to experience His Saving Work in us. And how do we experience His Saving Work in us?: through the Mass and the Seven Sacraments.

For example:

* Through the *Holy Sacrifice of the Mass*, Christ offers His Body

and Blood to God the Father as the Perfect Victim for all the sins of the whole world! And He offers that *Sacrifice* through the **Sacrament of the Priesthood** (Holy Orders)!

* Through the **Sacrament of the Eucharist**, our Lord *nourishes* us spiritually with His Body and Blood in Holy Communion, giving us Sanctifying Grace to enable us to grow in love and keep His Commandments.

* And as we said, through the **Sacrament of Matrimony**, Christ gives us His Grace/Help to fulfill the duties of married life as a husband or wife, father or mother.

- **Remaining In Christ's Grace**

Of course, it is necessary to remain in God's Grace throughout our lives. To be in the State of Mortal Sin radically breaks our union with Christ. Christ then no longer lives in us, nor do we live in Him. If a husband and/or wife is in a State of Mortal Sin, they should get out of it by *regretting* their sins and going to Confession (the **Sacrament of Penance**) as soon as possible. Through Confession, Christ acts to forgive men's sins. In that way they are returned to God's Grace/Help in fulfilling the duties of their married life. If the husband and wife are in God's Grace, Christ will live in them and they will live in Him, so intimately *united* will He be with them. Through the Mass and the Sacraments, Christ *acts* to make us holy!

- **Pure, Faithful, And True Love**

There is no greater blessing in married life than the pure, faithful and true love of a husband and wife. Their love must never fail; it must grow deeper and stronger day by day. All their activities must be guided by an unselfish spirit of perfect sacrifice; then they will experience the greatest measure of happiness possible in this world. Everything else is in God's hands. Through the Sacrament of Matrimony, God will be attentive to their needs and support them with His Graces. (See *Roman Ritual* 1964.)

- **A Null Attempt To Marry!**

Since marriage between a Baptized man and woman has been raised to the dignity of a Sacrament by Christ the Lord, marriage is, by its very nature, profoundly bound-up with our Holy Religion. Our Lord expects that we will obey His Church in all matters concerned with the practice of the Catholic Faith.

The Catholic Church is not only our Teacher, but also our Spiritual Mother; and like a Protective Mother, the Church has striven down through the centuries to safeguard the Sacrament of Marriage from the chaos and confusion of the world; and to protect her children from a tragic and wrongly-executed attempt to marry.

"Do What He Tells You"

So the Universal Laws of the Catholic Church require that – under ordinary circumstances – *every Catholic* man or woman must be married in the presence of a parish priest (or his delegate), and at least two witnesses (often, the designated "best man" and "maid of honor" serve that role).

- **No Marriage At All!**

Any attempt of a Catholic to marry in the presence of a Protestant minister or a "justice of the peace", or any other person *not officially delegated* by the Church, would render the "marriage" *null* and *void*. In other words, the couple would *not* be "getting married" *at all*! *No* **Marriage would actually be taking place in the sight of God *or man*!** A magnificent church building, grand organ music, toothy singers, tuxedos and gowns, flower girls and ring-bearers, ushers and bridesmaids, limousines or horse carriages, a grand wedding reception: and *still No Marriage* would be taking place at all! Not in the eyes of God or of His Church! The couple would simply ***not*** be married! Why? Because if *anyone* attempting marriage is a Catholic, they must marry as mentioned above, or there is *No Marriage*. Period. ***They are not married*!** And sad to say, if a Catholic *knows* this and does so anyway, he/she commits a Mortal Sin before God. And the fact remains: *They would not be Married*. The graces and blessings of Christ which they would have obtained through His Sacrament of Matrimony would not be there to assist the couple, since they would then be living together *outside of marriage*! And they would be living in Mortal Sin.

GROWING IN LOVE

- **"Till Death Do Us Part"**

I'm looking at a photo-portrait of a husband and wife in their very old age. The elderly husband is hugging his wife with a playful smile on his face as he looks toward the camera. The wife's smiling face reveals her delight in the affection he is showing to her. It is obvious that both are accustomed to these signs of affection for each other. They are unaware that in a few short months, he will go to God. Their marriage of 52 years is about to come to an end. But they are so happy together. It is as though the two of them have become like one person. Their love has grown ever deeper, over the many years of their marriage.

- **"I Thee Wed"**

Also on the wall, is their wedding picture. I see the groom standing there, dignified, young and strong; the bride, in her long white gown, is delicate and charming. They are smiling with a confidence founded on their devoted love for each other. They are happy in the total commitment they have made to share the joys and sorrows of life. They have vowed before God and man to be faithful and intimate friends for the whole of their life, helping each other to grow in holiness and love.

- **The Family**

Now my attention is drawn to another treasured picture in their home. It is a photo-portrait of their seven children...the fruit of their love...snuggled around their proud father and radiant mother: The Family! And the smiles on the faces of the father, mother, and children emote peace, joy, intimacy, and secure love.

- **In Good Times And In Bad**

At the beginning of the world, God told Adam and Eve – the first man and woman of the human race – to "increase and multiply". And they did "increase and multiply" – they did have children. But they also *sinned* against God, bringing down upon themselves – and their children, and their children's children, and the entire human race – a condition by which our minds have become darkened and our will power has become weak.

So marriages now have taken on the stresses and strains of life. In order to have a happy marriage, it takes effort, endurance, and self-sacrifice on our part. Even with the best of intentions, there are misunderstandings between us humans. We may "get on each other's nerves". We may have *personality* or *character* traits which grate on the sensibilities of other members of the family. Husbands and wives and their children may have to put-up with each other's *peculiarities* or *temperaments* over the years.

- **The Family Must Love And Care For Each Other**

The world outside your home will not care a bit about you or your family. In fact, the Worldlings don't even care about each other. The only people your family will be able to depend on will be the members of your family. If you don't love and care for one another, the world outside your door will not be eager to take up the slack.

A husband has to love and care for his wife; and a wife has to love and care for her husband. A mother and father have to love and care for their children; and the children must learn to love and care for their parents and their brothers and/or sisters.

Children are a gift
from the Lord;
the fruit of the womb
is a reward.

cf. Psalm 127

In the *Supernatural* realm – we belong to the Kingdom of God – we are members of a *loving* Communion of Saints. But in the *Natural* realm – we dwell in the Kingdom of man – where the only *loving* society you are apt to encounter is your family. If the members of your family don't care about each other...who will? Your home should be like a safe port in a raging storm, a haven of peace and love in a troubled world, a shelter and refuge from the chaotic winds of our times.

- **...In A Holy And Harmonious Home**

Pope Paul VI, in an allocution (formal address) given at Nazareth on January 5, 1964, urged that family members should live together in harmony and peace. They should encourage one another; be cheerful; and contribute to man's salvation through the *discipline* of hard, but healthful, work. Family members also need *spiritual discipline*: therefore, they should strive for holiness, while maintaining an atmosphere of silence in their home. A quiet home atmosphere will enable them to be steady in their good thoughts, inclined toward the interior things of the soul, and always ready to pay attention to the secret promptings of God and the instructions of true teachers. Family members also need – and should appreciate – the necessity of preparation, of study, of thinking about the things of God, and of engaging in that personal prayer which God alone sees.

Furthermore, the family should live as a community of love. The family is a beautiful, sacred, and inviolable way of life, of prime importance to the social order.

If the members of the family live in holiness, think in harmony, keep peace among themselves, and are attentive to each other's needs, they will experience a good measure of joy in this world, and eternal joy in Heaven.

WHEN YOU SAY: "I DO!"

At a Catholic Wedding, the groom and bride express their consent to marriage in these or similar words:

"(Groom's Name), do you take (Bride's Name) for your lawful wife, to have and to hold, from this day forward, for better, for worse, for richer, for poorer, in sickness and in health, until death do you part?"
The groom responds:
"I do."
Then the priest asks the bride:
"(Bride's Name), do you take (Groom's Name) for your lawful husband, to have and to hold, from this day forward, for better, for worse, for richer, for poorer, in sickness and in health, until death do you part?"

The bride responds:
"I do."

When both bride and groom pronounce these two words: **"I do"** – their marriage vows take effect. It is at that moment that they become *married for life.*

WHEN TO SAY: "I DON'T!"

However, during the Courtship ("steady - dating") period of a relationship, it may be necessary/crucial for the man or woman to say with finality: ***"I don't!"*** In other words: "This relationship is *over*!"

The moment to say: **"I don't!"** – is the moment when you discover that the person you are "steady - dating" exhibits one or another of the following traits:

◊ drinks alcohol to excess
◊ abuses drugs
◊ gambles heavily
◊ indulges in pornography
◊ flirts with others
◊ is given to rage; or violent outbursts
◊ is vengeful
◊ shows definite signs of being lazy, unconcerned about employment
◊ displays sullen moodiness; becomes uncommunicative
◊ is disposed to unexplained absences; secretive or puzzling behavior
◊ exhibits unjustified or unreasonable jealousy
◊ demands "sex-before-marriage" under threat of ending the relationship
◊ does not want children
◊ is juvenile in thinking and behavior
◊ relates very poorly and shows disrespect for parents
◊ abuses pets
◊ etc., etc., etc.

A DIFFICULT COURTSHIP

Courtship should be the happiest of times for a couple who have only recently discovered each other. If you are *already in tears* during your courtship, what will your marriage be like?

What will the Marriage be like?

If you are in *tears* **before** the wedding, you'll be in *torrents* **after**! Such marriages end up in bitter civil divorces a few years later, and leave deep emotional scars on the children. Children from broken homes suffer profound and notable unhappiness; are prone to sexual promiscuity, lack of motivation, discontentment, and feelings of intense, unrelenting neediness. Children in such situations are also inclined to fall into criminal behavior such as: drug abuse, perversity, petty thievery, drunkenness, and intense rage.

◊ Rather than suffer a bad marriage, *terminate* the engagement while you still have the right to do so. The best barometer for a joyful marriage is a joyful courtship! Marriage is supposed to be a life-long friendship! You don't inflict hardship on your friend. Certainly, one of the greatest "friendships" should be the friendship between a husband and wife!

◊ Don't allow yourself to be talked-into renewing your courtship by pledges and promises of future good behavior by the offender.

◊ Usher him/her out the nearest door and wave a final goodbye. If your fiancé has not grown-up or overcome such deficiencies in 21 years (or so) of life, he/she will not do so in the few months remaining before the wedding. It is *too late* at this point to *prove* that his/her life is *really* changed, just because he/she is on "good behavior" for a few months before marriage.

◊ It is presumed that a man and woman intending to make a life-long commitment to marriage are *mature* and *responsible* enough to do so, **before** they begin steady-dating.

◊ When it comes down to a *decision* on whether or not to *commit* yourself to someone for life, it is wise to follow the same Principle you employ when unsure of the freshness of something in your refrigerator: "When in doubt, throw it out!"

"MY LOVE WILL CHANGE HIM/HER…"

It's a sad and unfortunate mistake to think that:

"My Love will change him/her after we're married."

That false idea has led to *thousands* of failed marriages each year. It simply doesn't work out that way. Instead, be grateful to God that you recognize these dangerous traits *before* getting married! And don't hesitate for one moment to break-off your relationship *then* and there – *before* you become too emotionally involved. If you are *already* emotionally involved, struggle with all your might to break the engagement *immediately*. Difficult as this may be, it's better than undergoing undue suffering, conflict, misery, and distress throughout the years of your marriage.

Let there be no wavering on your part. Take the nearest exit ramp off the "Sad-Life Highway" before your bumpy courtship turns into a rocky marriage. Agreeing to marry such a person may *temporarily* fulfill your "need", but it will *not* fulfill "love". There is a world of difference between "loving" and "needing". If he/she is "*one* in a million", take consolation in the fact that there are many millions to choose "one" from!

AVOIDING THE NEAR OCCASIONS FOR RUINING A LOVING MARRIAGE

Our Lord says:

"You have heard that it was said, 'You shall not commit adultery.' But I say to you that every one who looks at a woman lustfully has already committed adultery with her in his heart. If your right eye is an occasion of sin for you, pluck it out and cast it away from you; it is better for you to lose part of your body than to have your whole body cast into Hell. And if your right hand is an occasion of sin for you, cut it off and cast it away; it is better for you to lose one of your limbs than to have your whole body cast into Hell."

(Matthew 5:27-30)

The graphic imagery of Christ's solemn words is not to be taken literally...the early followers of our Lord did not go around plucking-out their eyes and cutting-off their hands...; rather they understood that Jesus was emphasizing a crucial fact:

- **Avoid The Near Occasions Of Sin!**

A husband and wife must *avoid* any person, place, or thing that would lead them to violate their loving marriage. There are countless occasions and situations which could lead a husband or wife to *sin* against their marriage, destroying their loving relationship for each other. A few examples may be helpful:

◊ A wife or husband discussing a marriage problem with a friend (whose own marriage has been civilly terminated by divorce), rather than "talk it out" with her/his spouse at an opportune time. (An "opportune time" would *not* be when emotions are running high! It may be hours, days, weeks, or months later!)

Other "Occasions of Sin" against a marriage would be:

◊ A husband taking his secretary out to lunch and a ride in the countryside, and a "chat" at a motel room.

◊ A wife inviting the man next door over to her house for coffee while her husband is at work.

◊ A husband frequenting a tavern after work, in order to "dialogue" and dance with any female who happens to be sitting at the end of the bar.

◊ Keeping company with immoral or irreligious "friends".

◊ Etc., Etc., Etc., Etc., Etc., Etc., Etc., Etc., Etc., Etc., Etc. (I'm aware that there are not enough "Etceteras" – but I get tired.)

◊ (Perhaps you may be inclined to add a few examples yourself.)

- **Sins Against Marriage**

The Sixth Commandment of God demands

"You shall not sin against marriage"

◊ **Adultery Violates Marriage**

No one should attempt to be alone with, or attempt to date, or seduce, or engage in sexual activity with another's husband or wife. And certainly, no wife or husband should attempt to obtain a civil divorce in order to "marry" someone else. (In God's eyes, *no one* can terminate a valid marriage!)

◊ **Fornication (And Sins Related To Fornication)**

Sexual sins between unmarried persons likewise violate the meaning of marriage, and do not serve to prepare them for a successful marriage in the future. Indulging in such sins retards the spiritual, mental, and emotional growth necessary to contract a happy, holy marriage. Among the sins committed outside marriage are:

√ prolonged, sexually-motivated embraces
√ sensuous kisses
√ passionate caressing
√ sexually suggestive conversations, postures, gestures
√ immodesty in dress
√ gazing lustfully at others

√   sexual self-abuse

These sins pervert the true *meaning* of marriage as a *loving union* between a husband and wife. Such sins also trivialize the true *purpose* of marriage, which is to *procreate children* through that *loving union*. Sad to say, such sinful acts as those mentioned above are neither *loving* nor *procreative*, but rather self-centered and barren.

◊   **Sinful Birth Control**

A fruit tree – by its very nature – is meant to bear fruit! Our Lord once *condemned* a fig tree because it did *not* bear fruit! The fig tree did not fulfill its *meaning* and *purpose*; the fig tree was meant to blossom-forth, for the purpose of bearing fruit; and this it did not do. The fig tree violated its reason for existing; it did not do what it was supposed to do as a fruit tree!

It is very similar with marriage – although there are differences. A fig tree has only one purpose: to bear figs. A marriage has *two* purposes – a primary purpose and a secondary purpose. Primarily marriage is for the procreation and education of children; secondarily, marriage is for the mutual love between the spouses. However, there are instances when God will not choose to give children to this or that marriage; but this marriage is just as much a Sacrament and a means of Grace as the marriage of those who are blessed with many children! God still requires that the husband and wife should fulfill the meaning and purpose of loving each other. However, when a husband and wife express their love through the marital act, they must be *open* to the possibility of producing new life (a child!) as the fruit of their love. No married couple is permitted by God to employ any method devised to obstruct the procreation of children (if God should choose to give them such a gift!).

So, any attempt to thwart the *meaning* and *purpose* of marriage by sinful birth-control, violates marriage itself, violates its very reason for existing. Such a marriage does *not do* what it is supposed to be *open* to doing – it is *not open* to bringing forth children as the fruit of a loving union between a husband and wife.

The Sixth Commandment of God demands that we must not sin against marriage. God condemns any sinful, unnatural attempts to prevent the conception and consequent birth of a child: methods such as:

- √ condoms
- √ premature withdrawal (a form of masturbation)
- √ the mutilation of one's healthy reproductive organs by direct surgical sterilization (male vasectomy or female tubal ligation, etc.)
- √ the use of Norplant
- √ R. U. 46
- √ antiseptic douches
- √ contraceptive pills
- √ diaphragms
- √ foams
- √ gels
- √ spermicides
- √ suppositories
- √ cervical caps
- √ sponges

and the like (Did I miss any?), are repulsive to God and invite His Wrath. (It's worth noting that the contraceptive "Pill" and assorted other methods of sinful birth-control often serve to induce the abortion-murder of an already conceived human being at the very beginning of its life.)

- • **Mortal Sin And Marriage Are Not Compatible**

If the occasions for committing Mortal Sin are *not avoided*, we risk the eternal loss of the Kingdom of Heaven...and our stay here on Earth will not be very pleasant either! Mortal Sin does *not* promote love for God or man. Behind every broken or unhappy marriage, you will find *sin* lurking in the shadows. Find the *sin* (or sins) and you've found the problem. *Conquer* the sin and you've conquered the problem. *Nothing* ruins a loving marriage but *sin*. "Mortal Sins do not a happy marriage make." Keep Mortal Sin *out* of your marriage.

Mortal Sins committed against a spouse bring the marriage to its *Lowest* Level of Love – while instigating a *High* Level of Hate. And the offense of *sin* is not only in the *doing*; but also in the "setting-up" for *doing*: by placing oneself in a *situation* whereby Mortal Sin is easily committed against a husband or wife.

If your marriage and family life are to have any measure of happiness and holiness, **Mortal Sin** must be out of the picture. Mortal Sin drove the nails and pierced the heart of Christ! If you are not at peace with God, you will not be at peace with yourself. And if you are not at peace with yourself, you will not be at peace with your spouse.

- **Deliberate Venial Sin**

Venial Sins should not be taken too lightly either:

Venial sins against a husband or wife *lower* the Level of Love in a marriage. So it is a mistake to look at our Venial Vices as though they were some sort of "Inviolable Virtues"!:

◊ "She knew I had a bad temper before she married me!...So she'll have to get used to it!"

◊ "He knows I get sarcastic and spiteful when I don't get my way...he'll have to learn to accept it!"

It's one thing to be grumpy on a given occasion. It's another thing to enter into a partnership with your grumpiness! It's one thing to have a "short fuse." It's another thing to say "Well, that's the way I am!"...and to treat it as though it were some Fashionable Character Trait!

- **Sins Of Omission Or Neglect**

When a man and woman consent to marriage at their wedding, they are giving and accepting the rights to each other's bodies for acts *open* to the procreation of children (marital intercourse). Therefore, it would be mortally sinful for either the husband or wife to refuse to render that marital debt when their spouse reasonably requests it. God tells us through the pen of St. Paul that:

> *"the husband must give his wife what she has a right to expect, and so too the wife to the husband. The wife has no rights over her own body; it is the husband who has them. In the same way, the husband has no rights over his body; the wife has them. Do not refuse each other except by mutual consent, and then only for an agreed time, to leave yourselves for prayer; then come together again in case Satan should take advantage of your weakness to tempt you."*
> *(1 Corinthians 7:4-5) Jerusalem Bible Translation*

Of course, husbands and wives likewise have the right to expect from their spouse:

√ due attention

√ cooperation
√ affection
√ patience

- **Hurtful Words**

There are so many ways to offend those we love. And those ways should be avoided like an infectious disease. For example, great damage is done to a loving relationship when harsh words are spoken:

"You make me sick!"
"I regret the day I married you!"
"I hate you!"
"What did I ever see in you!"
"Damn you!"
"You disgust me!"
"Go to hell!"

Such hurtful words are like arrows in the heart, which remain there forever. They deeply wound the love which should be the heart of every marriage. The only way to remove such arrows is by deep-felt repentance on the part of the offender; and a profound apology accompanied by a firm resolve **never** to act that way again; and then, in fact, such an offense must *never* happen again!…**"Go, and sin no more"**!

WEALTH AND LUXURY ARE NOT WHAT MARRIAGE IS

Wealth and luxury do not guarantee a happy, loving, marriage. In recent years, the Worldlings have been peddling a *package of woes* for young married couples, and unfortunately, too many newlyweds have bought it.

- **False Notions**

Too many married people have bought *false notions* such as:
  ◊ "There should be no more than *two* children in a family. That's going to give you freedom; that's going to give you the good things of life – the education, lots of toys, a boat, a second home, designer clothing – you name it!"
  ◊ "Experience *everything* in life! Have a boat, have a sports car, have a dog, have a cat, maybe even have a 'kid' (preferably of the goat variety)!"

But the only problem is that after they have all these "things" of life…after they do it all…they end up *divorced*! And *hating* each other! Their marriage and family are ruined!

Marriage and family life don't work that way. Both marriage and family are *destroyed* by the time they would have really *enjoyed* it! They've bought the worldly package. They've *bought the lie*. The Worldlings told them what they were expected to do, and they went out and did it. Now, it is a few years later, and their marriage is on the rocks, and they've lost all the *children* they could have had; they've lost all the *happiness* they could have had...as husband and wife, as father and mother. Now that they're old enough to know that they have been duped...it is too late! They can't have children any more. Their age has rendered them barren; or they are barren because they have presented themselves to a surgeon to be "spayed" like the family cat (by means of a tubal ligation, vasectomy, or other method of *mutilating* their healthy reproductive system). Thus, their union will bring them no more children. They were snookered by the lie and thought that was the way they should go.

- **Troubled Children**

The one or two children they produced learned to be self-centered and pleasure-seeking. Education seems unimportant to them. They never seem to have enough toys and joys. The package of woes their parents have mistakenly bought is not what their children want or need.

Their children need a true family; they need a father and mother who have not artlessly and selfishly limited their family to one or two children. They don't need their brothers and sisters murdered by abortion. They don't care about the boat and the vacation home. They see that their parents have failed. They realize that what their parents chose as a lifestyle and belief-system was wrong! The failure of their parents' marriage and the unhappiness and loneliness of their dysfunctional family has unwrapped the *package of lies* their parents have bought, and the children don't like the evil they see inside. They have an innate sense that marriage is not merely Material, but also Spiritual.

- **But Marriage Does Need Money**

However, your Marriage will need more than love and the air that you breathe to survive. We live in a physical world. In order to survive, we need food, clothing, and a roof over our head to protect us from excessive heat or cold. Additional needs arise when one or another member of the family requires medical attention as well. Marriage can't survive on "love" alone.

"Through the work
of your hands you will eat"

- **Husband And Father**

Therefore, it is necessary for the groom to be employed in some career, business, or occupation which earns enough money or goods to support a wife and family. The proper time for a man to learn a trade or obtain an education so that he may be gainfully employed is *before* he attempts to seek a woman to marry. If he determines that, as yet, he would not be able to provide for the basic needs of a wife and at least his first child, he is not in a position to get married.

It is unfair to expect a wife and mother to be away from home and working at a job, while at the same time she is supposed to be raising the children with proper care and attention and attending to the well-being of her husband. Not only will the family be neglected, but her own physical and emotional health, and her spiritual well-being will be jeopardized.

- **Wife And Mother**

It happens more often than not that God calls on a wife and mother to give birth to several or more children (the average woman is physically capable of bearing fourteen children). It would then be the task of the husband and father to support and provide-for the physical, emotional, spiritual, and financial needs of his family. This necessitates that he must work to earn a livelihood, while his wife – in the normal course of things – will bear the children. And it is the *wife* who will be their mother! Her *power* and *influence* in this world resides in the fact that, as a mother, she will form and shape the future of Society through her children! The character and moral fiber of a Nation is dependent on the influence of mothers on their children!

The importance of a wife and mother does not rest on her ability to exercise "executive power" over ten people at the office; her mission in life is not in being an Office Manager!

A wife and mother already has a full-time job in caring for her children...and her husband! (As the saying goes: "Behind every great man is a great woman!").

On Judgment Day, God is not going to ask a father or mother how high he/she climbed in their workaday careers; nor how high they climbed in Society. Rather, God will ask them what kind of father or mother they were...what kind of husband or wife! It is in the school called The Family that a child learns from his/her parents what it is to be a man, husband, and father, or a woman, wife, and mother.

May
your wife
be like a
fruitful vine;
and your children
like olive plants
around
your table

THE CHALLENGES AND BLESSINGS OF MARRIAGE

Through the Sacrament of Matrimony, a Baptized man and woman undertake a profoundly important mission in life. They have a vocation from God – a "special calling" from God to serve Him as husband and wife in their roles as spouse and parent.

And God knows that they will not be able to fulfill their mission without His help. He promises them His assistance throughout the years of their married life. He enables them to carry out their mission – as husband and wife, father and mother – through the Grace of the Sacrament of Matrimony, which they embraced on the day of their wedding. Likewise, through the Mass and the Sacraments (Confession, Holy Communion, etc.), Christ Jesus will carry out His Saving Work in them, in good times and in bad, as they journey together through life.

Not only will they enjoy their gift of themselves to each other as intimate companions in marriage; but also (if God so wills it), they will be blessed with children – sprung from their loving union. Christ will give them enabling Grace to see God in each other and in their children. Consecrating themselves to the Eternal God, they must serve Him every day in many ordinary ways, and teach their children to do the same.

Then, the love shared between the husband and wife and their offspring will bless them with as much happiness as can be experienced in this "valley of tears." And our Lord assures them that they will receive immeasurable happiness and eternal life *forever* in Heaven!

THE
WEDDING

CHAPTER IV
THE WEDDING CEREMONY:

A SPIRITUAL AND RELIGIOUS REALITY

As I mentioned earlier, there are, at times, *physical* and *emotional* experiences in marriage; but marriage is essentially a *spiritual* and *religious* reality. After all, God Himself is the Author of marriage.

I also pointed out that marriage is – by its very nature – an *unbreakable* and *exclusive* union of love and fidelity, shared between a man and a woman for the primary purpose of procreating and educating their children. And there is a very important *secondary* purpose: the emotional, physical, mental, social, economic, and spiritual well-being of the spouses through a freely contracted bond of love!

THE SACRAMENT OF MARRIAGE

I also noted that when a marriage is contracted by a *baptized* man and a *baptized* woman, Christ the Lord raises that marriage to the sacred dignity of a Sacrament! Through the Holy Sacrament of Matrimony, the husband and wife become an effective *sign* and *expression* of Christ's loving and unbreakable union with His Mystical Body the Church.

Likewise, through that Holy Sacrament of Marriage, Christ gives His Grace/Help to the married couple, in order to assist them in carrying-out the duties and obligations of their marriage vows.

The Sacrament of Matrimony, then, is a profound *spiritual* and *religious* event which takes place in the presence of God and man. Therefore it would be a gross contradiction for that husband and wife – after their wedding – not to practice the Religion of God in which they were s*acramentally* married in Christ.

PREPARING FOR YOUR MARRIAGE

The Roman Catholic Church, which receives its authority from Christ the Lord Himself, has certain general requirements which must be fulfilled in order to marry validly.

Likewise, the local parish church where you will exchange your marriage vows, will also have some particular preparations which will be necessary before the wedding.

In order to meet the general requirements of the Church, certain documents must be provided and presented to the parish priest (A pastor may at times delegate a Deacon to officiate at a wedding):

"I Thee Wed"

- **For Roman Catholics:**
    * A recent copy of your Baptismal Certificate dated and issued within six months of your wedding date.
    * An old or new copy of your First Communion and Confirmation certificates.
- **For Baptized Christians:**
    * An old or new copy of your Baptismal Certificate.
- **Civil Requirements:**
    * A valid Civil License for Marriage must be obtained from the Town in which the marriage is to take place. (This requirement may differ in various states.)
    * That Civil License, with the envelope in which the License was obtained, is to be presented to the priest at the wedding rehearsal.
    * A Marriage License is valid only for a limited time from the Date of Application. Contact the local Town Clerk's Office to verify the procedures and requirements for obtaining a Marriage License.
- **Your Diocese May Require:**
    * That you attend an Engaged Couples Conference, and/or that you participate in some pre-marriage program or inventory.
- **The Wedding Event:**
    * For Catholics who are living a sacramental way of life, a Wedding Mass is preferable and commendable.
    * For Catholics who do *not* regularly attend Mass or receive the Sacraments (Confession, Holy Communion, etc.) a wedding ceremony *without* a Mass should be celebrated.
    * For a mixed marriage between a Catholic and one who is of another faith, it is customary to celebrate a wedding ceremony *without* Mass.
- **Your Wedding Mass Selections:**
    * The wedding couple may wish to select Wedding Mass A, B, or C, to be celebrated by the priest; or, they may choose from any of the Prayers in sets A, B, or C interchangeably. These selections may be found on pages 76 through 89 in this book.

* The couple may also choose the Wedding Mass Readings. These may be proclaimed by designated Catholic readers. These selections may be found on pages 91 through 111 in this book.
* The groom and bride may also decide to leave these selections to the priest.

- **Vows:**
  * The couple must select one of the options provided on pages 129 through 130. ˈ
  (Note: A pull-out form is provided at the back of this book, to be presented to the priest, to indicate your preferences.)

- **"Unity" Candle, Flowers, Confetti, Wedding Carpet/Runners, Libations, Etc.:**
  * Check with the priest regarding "do's" and "don'ts" for weddings in the parish.

- **Music:**
  * The solemnity of the Sacrament of Matrimony calls for sacred music appropriate for a wedding. *Other selections of music, while popular and even well-composed in themselves, are more suitable for a wedding reception than for a church ceremony.* The parish music director should be consulted about your sacred music preferences. Of course, the pastor of the parish is the final authority in deciding what music is appropriate for a Catholic wedding ceremony.

- **Offering:**
  * A specified monetary offering is given to the parish for the wedding. The offering covers costs for the priest; the organist's fee; heat, lighting, air-conditioning expenses; janitorial service; etc.
  * The offering may be presented along with the Marriage License at the time of the wedding rehearsal.
  * Check with the priest regarding the amount of the offering.

- **Pictures, Videos, Etc.:**
  * The photographer and/or videographer should check with the priest/celebrant just before the wedding ceremony to discuss what is permitted.

- **The Rehearsal:**
  - * Arrange a date and time for the wedding rehearsal with the priest, since it is he who conducts the rehearsal.
  - * Decide before the rehearsal the order and pairing of ushers and bridesmaids. The priest will do the rest.
  - * If everyone, including the bride and attendants, arrives promptly for the rehearsal, it should take only about 45 minutes, and you can arrange your rehearsal dinner accordingly.

- **Marriage Records:**
  - * At the end of the marriage ceremony, the priest will hand you a legal Marriage Certificate as proof of your marriage in the Catholic Church.
  - * Your Civil License will be signed and mailed to the Town Clerk's Office within days of the wedding. If you wish to obtain a certified copy, it can be obtained there.

- **Spiritual Preparation:**
  - * "Behold, I make all things new," said the Lord. And, in fact, He has raised *natural* marriage to a new *supernatural* level, elevating it to unimaginable heights and profound dignity by making it one of the Seven Sacraments. This means that a Sacramental Christian Marriage between a baptized man and baptized woman is radically different and supremely sublime compared to a *natural* marriage between unbaptized persons.

THREE TO GET MARRIED

A Sacramental Marriage is a community of three: the husband, the wife, and Christ; and that community is a community of love...*through* Christ, *with* Christ, and *in* Christ! When a Sacramental Marriage is lived in *love*, it brings about the sanctification of the married couple and makes-present in this world the loving, exclusive and permanent union of Christ with His Mystical Body: the Church.

These facts suggest that the groom and bride should strive – throughout their life – to live in God's Grace. Regular attendance at Mass on *all* Sundays and Holydays of Obligation and frequent participation in the Sacrament of Confession (Penance) would be essential for the forgiveness of sins, grace, and the Glory of God.

- **Before The Wedding**

The couple soon to be married should go to Confession on the weekend before their wedding, and continue to do so *frequently* and *regularly* throughout the years of their life. Truly blessed are those children who – from their earliest years – see their father and mother on their knees, going to Confession, and are taught by their parents to do the same.

It is appropriate and well-advised for the Catholic Best Man and Maid of Honor to go to Confession at least on the weekend before the wedding.

Likewise, if the wedding ceremony is to be celebrated within a Mass, only those *Catholics* who are *properly* and *spiritually* prepared should come forward to receive Christ Jesus in Holy Communion.

Holy Communion is distributed by the priest and/or deacon, assisted if necessary, by a duly commissioned extraordinary minister of Holy Communion.

FURTHER QUESTIONS?

Although I have covered a number of items here, there may be other questions and requests which need an answer. Feel perfectly free to discuss them with your priest, who will be anxious to do all that is permissible to make your holy wedding day a joyous one.

THE ORDER OF MASS FOR MARRIAGE

- Procession of the Bridal Party And Bride
- Opening Prayer (Priest)
- Reading I: From The Old Testament (Lay Reader)
- Responsorial Psalm (Lay Reader or Organist)
- Reading II: From The New Testament (Lay Reader)
- Gospel Acclamation: Verse And Response (Lay Reader or Organist/ Soloist)
- Gospel Reading (Priest)
- Homily/Sermon (Priest)
- Consent To Marriage: Wedding Vows (Groom And Bride)
- Blessing Of Ring(s) (Priest)
- Exchange Of Rings (Groom And Bride)
- General Intercessions/Prayer Of The Faithful (Lay Reader)
- Offertory (Priest)
- Prayer Over The Gifts (Priest)
- The Preface (Priest)
- The Eucharistic Prayer (Priest)
- The Lord's Prayer (Priest And People)
- Nuptial Blessing Of The Groom And Bride (Priest)
- Reception Of Holy Communion (Catholic Faithful)
- Prayer After Communion (Priest)
- Solemn Blessing Of The Groom And Bride And Then The People (Priest)
- Dismissal (Priest)

WEDDING MASS

PRAYERS:

On the following pages you may select *one* of the complete sets of Wedding Mass Prayers:

        Set A
        Set B
        Set C

or you may choose from any set interchangeably:

        one **Opening Prayer**
        one **Prayer Over The Gifts**
        one **Prayer After Communion**

WEDDING MASS

PRAYERS:

Selection A

Introductory Rites

May the Lord send you help from his holy place and from Zion may he watch over you. May he grant you your heart's desire and lend his aid to all your plans.   *(Ps 19:3,5)*

Opening Prayer

Father,
You have made the bond of marriage
a holy mystery,
a symbol of Christ's love for his Church.
Hear our prayers for N. and N.
With faith in you and in each other
they pledge their love today.
May their lives always bear witness
to the reality of that love.

We ask this through our Lord Jesus Christ, your
     Son,
who lives and reigns with you and the Holy
     Spirit,
one God, for ever and ever.

OR:

Father,
when you created mankind
you willed that man and wife should be one.
Bind N. and N.
in the loving union of marriage
and make their love fruitful
so that they may be living witnesses
to your divine love in the world.

77

We ask this through our Lord Jesus Christ, your
Son,
who lives and reigns with you and the Holy
Spirit,
one God, for ever and ever.

*See Selections of **Readings**, on pages 91 through 128*

Prayer Over   Pray, brethren...
The Gifts

Lord,
accept our offering
for this newly married couple, N. and N.
By your love and providence you have brought
them together;
now bless them all the days of their married life.

We ask this through Christ our Lord.

*See **Preface of Marriage**, Selection nos. I - II - III, pages 134 through 136*

When Eucharistic Prayer I is used, the special form of **Father, accept this**
offering *is said. The words in brackets may be omitted if desired.*

Father, accept this offering
from your whole family
and from N. and N., for whom we now pray.
You have brought them to their wedding day:
grant them (the gift and joy of children and)
a long and happy life together.

[Through Christ our Lord. Amen.]

Nuptial Blessing
With hands joined, the priest says:

My dear friends, let us turn to the Lord and pray
that he will bless with his grace this woman
(or N.)
now married in Christ to this man (or N.)
and that (through the sacrament of the body and
blood of Christ)

he will unite in love the couple he has joined in
this holy bond.

*All pray silently for a short while. Then the priest extends his hands and
continues:*

Father,
by your power you have made everything out of
nothing.
In the beginning you created the universe
and made mankind in your own likeness.

You gave man the constant help of woman
so that man and woman should no longer be two,
but one flesh,
and you teach us that what you have united
may never be divided.

Father,
by your plan man and woman are united,
and married life has been established
as the one blessing that was not forfeited by
original sin
or washed away in the flood.

Look with love upon this woman, your daughter,
now joined to her husband in marriage.
She asks your blessing.
Give her the grace of love and peace.
May she always follow the example of the holy
women
whose praises are sung in the scriptures.

May her husband put his trust in her
and recognize that she is his equal
and the heir with him to the life of grace.
May he always honor her and love her
as Christ loves his bride, the Church.

Father,
keep them always true to your commandments.

Keep them faithful in marriage
and let them be living examples of Christian life.

Give them the strength which comes from the
        gospel
so that they may be witnesses of Christ to others.
[Bless them with children
and help them to be good parents.
May they live to see their children's children.]
And, after a happy old age,
grant them fullness of life with the saints
in the kingdom of heaven.

We ask this through Christ our Lord.

The Mass continues in the usual way.

Communion Rite   Christ loves his Church, and he sacrificed himself for her so that she could become like a holy and untouchable bride.
                                (See Eph. 5:25-27.)

Prayer After   Let us pray.
Communion   *Pause for silent prayer, if this has not preceded.*
                   Lord,
                   in your love
                   you have given us this eucharist
                   to unite us with one another and with you.
                   As you have made N. and N.
                   one in this sacrament of marriage
                   (and in the sharing of the one bread and the one
                           cup),
                   so now make them one in love for each other.

                   We ask this through Christ our Lord.

Solemn Blessing God the eternal Father keep you in love with
                           each other,
                   so that the peace of Christ may stay with you
                   and be always in your home.
                   ℟. Amen.

May (your children bless you,)
your friends console you
and all men live in peace with you.
℟. Amen.

May you always bear witness to the love of God
      in this world
so that the afflicted and the needy
will find in you generous friends
and welcome you into the joys of heaven.
℟. Amen.

May almighty God bless you,
the Father, and the Son, and the Holy Spirit.
℟. Amen.

WEDDING MASS

PRAYERS:

Selection B

Introductory Rites

Fill us with your love, O Lord, and we will sing for joy all our days. May the goodness of the Lord be upon us, and give success to the work of our hands. *(Ps 89:14, 17)*

Opening Prayer

Father,
hear our prayers for N. and N.,
who today are united in marriage before your
    altar.
Give them your blessing,
and strengthen their love for each other.

We ask this through our Lord Jesus Christ, your
    Son,
who lives and reigns with you and the Holy
    Spirit,
one God, for ever and ever.

*See Selections of **Readings**, pages 91 through 128*

Prayer Over The Gifts

Pray brethren...

Lord,
accept the gifts we offer you
on this happy day.
In your fatherly love
watch over and protect N. and N.,
whom you have united in marriage.

We ask this through Christ our Lord.

*See **Preface of Marriage**, Selection nos. I - II - III, pages 134 through 136*

When Eucharistic Prayer I is used, the special form of **Father, accept this offering** *is said. The words in brackets may be omitted if desired.*

Father, accept this offering
from your whole family
and from N. and N., for whom we now pray.
You have brought them to their wedding day:
grant them (the gift and joy of children and)
a long and happy life together.

[Through Christ our Lord. Amen.]

Nuptial Blessing
With hands joined, the priest says:

Let us pray to the Lord for N. and N.
who come to God's altar at the beginning of their
     married life
so that they may always be united in love for
     each other
(as they now share in the body and blood of
     Christ).

All pray silently for a short while. The priest extends his hands and continues:

Holy Father, you created mankind in your own
     image
and made man and woman to be joined as
     husband and wife
in union of body and heart
and so fulfill their mission in this world.

Father,
to reveal the plan of your love,
you made the union of husband and wife
an image of the covenant between you and your
     people.
In the fulfillment of this sacrament,
the marriage of Christian man and woman
is a sign of the marriage between Christ and the
     Church.
Father, stretch out your hand, and bless N. and
N.

Lord,
grant that as they begin to live this sacrament
they may share with each other the gifts of your
    love
and become one in heart and mind
as witnesses to your presence in their marriage.
Help them to create a home together
(and give them children to be formed by the
    gospel
and to have a place in your family).

Give your blessings to N., your daughter,
so that she may be a good wife (and mother),
caring for the home,
faithful in love for her husband,
generous and kind.
Give your blessings to N., your son,
so that he may be a faithful husband
(and a good father).

Father,
grant that as they come together to your table on
    earth,
so they may one day have the joy of sharing your
    feast in heaven.

We ask this through Christ our Lord.

The Mass continues in the usual way.

Communion Rite	I give you a new commandment: love one another as I have loved you, says the Lord.
	(Jn 13:34)

Prayer After	Let us pray.
Communion	*Pause for silent prayer, if this has not preceded.*
	Lord,
	we who have shared the food of your table
	pray for our friends N. and N.,
	whom you have joined together in marriage.
	Keep them close to you always.

May their love for each other
proclaim to all the world
their faith in you.

We ask this through Christ our Lord.

Solemn Blessing   May God, the almighty Father,
give you his joy
and bless you (in your children).
℞ Amen.

May the only Son of God have mercy on you
and help you in good times and in bad.
℞ Amen.

May the Holy Spirit of God
always fill your hearts with his love.
℞ Amen.

May almighty God bless you,
the Father, and the Son, and the Holy Spirit.
℞ Amen.

WEDDING MASS

PRAYERS:

Selection C

Introductory Rites

Lord, I will bless you day after day, and praise your name for ever; for you are kind to all, and compassionate to all your creatures.

(Ps 144:2, 9.)

Opening Prayer

Almighty God,
hear our prayers for N. and N.,
who have come here today
to be united in the sacrament of marriage.
Increase their faith in you and in each other,
and through them bless your Church
(with Christian children).

We ask this through our Lord Jesus Christ, your
    Son,
who lives and reigns with you and the Holy
    Spirit,
one God, for ever and ever.

*See Selections of **Readings**, pages 91 through 128*

Prayer Over The Gifts

Pray, brethren...

Lord,
hear our prayers
and accept the gifts we offer for N. and N.
Today you have made them one in the sacrament
    of marriage.
May the mystery of Christ's unselfish love,
which we celebrate in this eucharist,
increase their love for you and for each other.

We ask this through Christ our Lord.

*See **Preface of Marriage**, Selections nos. I - II - III, pages 134 through 136*

When Eucharistic Prayer I is used, the special form of **Father, accept this offering** *is said. The words in brackets may be omitted if desired.*

Father, accept this offering
from your whole family
and from N. and N., for whom we now pray.
You have brought them to their wedding day:
grant them (the gift and joy of children and)
a long and happy life together.

[Through Christ our Lord. Amen.]

Nuptial Blessing

After the Lord's Prayer, the prayer **Deliver us** *is omitted. The priest faces the bride and bridegroom and says the following blessing over them:*

My dear friends, let us ask God
for his continued blessings upon this bridegroom
and his bride (or N. and N.).

All pray silently for a short while. Then the priest extends his hands and continues:

Holy Father,
creator of the universe,
maker of man and woman in your own likeness,
source of blessing for married life,
we humbly pray to you for this woman
who today is united with her husband in this
**   sacrament of marriage.**

May your fullest blessing come upon her and her
**   husband**
so that they may together rejoice in your gift of
**   married love**
(and enrich your Church with their children).

Lord,
may they both praise you when they are happy
and turn to you in their sorrows.

May they be glad that you help them in their
    work
and know that you are with them in their need.
May they pray to you in the community of the
    Church,
and be your witnesses in the world.
May they reach old age in the company of their
    friends,
and come at last to the kingdom of heaven.

We ask this through Christ our Lord.

The Mass continues in the usual way.

Communion Rite   I will bless the Lord at all times, his praise shall
be ever on my lips. Taste and see the goodness of
the Lord; blessed is he who hopes in God.
(Ps 33:1, 9)

Prayer After   Let us pray.
Communion   *Pause for silent prayer if this has not preceded.*
Almighty God,
may the sacrifice we have offered
and the eucharist we have shared
strengthen the love of N. and N.,
and give us all your fatherly aid.

We ask this through Christ our Lord.

Solemn Blessing   May the Lord Jesus, who was a guest at the
    wedding in Cana,
bless you and your families and friends.
℟. Amen.

May Jesus, who loved his Church to the end,
always fill your hearts with his love.
℟. Amen.

May he grant that, as you believe in his
    resurrection,
so you may wait for him in joy and hope.
℟. Amen.

May almighty God bless you,
the Father, and the Son, and the Holy Spirit.
℟. Amen.

WEDDING MASS

READINGS:

On the following pages you may select *one* Reading from each of the categories listed below, to be read at your Wedding Mass:

> *one* **Old Testament** Reading and/or
> *one* **New Testament** Reading
>
> *one* **Responsorial Psalm**
> *one* **Alleluia Verse** and **Verse Before the Gospel**
> *one* **Gospel** Reading

801* READINGS FROM THE OLD TESTAMENT
(choose one)

Selection #1

Male and female he created them.

A reading from the Book of Genesis   1:26-28, 31a

Then God said:
"Let us make man in our image, after our likeness.
Let them have dominion over the fish of the sea,
      the birds of the air, and the cattle,
      and over all the wild animals
      and all the creatures that crawl on the ground."

God created man in his image;
      in the image of God he created him;
      male and female he created them.

God blessed them, saying:
      "Be fertile and multiply;
      fill the earth and subdue it.
Have dominion over the fish of the sea, the birds of the air,
      and all the living things that move on the earth."
God looked at everything he had made, and he found it very good.

The word of the Lord.

* Number in the Lectionary

Selection #2

The two of them become one body.

A reading from the Book of Genesis   2:18-24

The LORD God said: "It is not good for the man to be alone.
I will make a suitable partner for him."
So the LORD God formed out of the ground
     various wild animals and various birds of the air,
     and he brought them to the man to see what he would call them;
     whatever the man called each of them would be its name.
The man gave names to all the cattle,
     all the birds of the air, and all wild animals;
     but none proved to be the suitable partner for the man.

So the LORD God cast a deep sleep on the man,
     and while he was asleep,
     he took out one of his ribs and closed up its place with flesh.
The LORD God then built up into a woman the rib
     that he had taken from the man.
When he brought her to the man, the man said:

     "This one, at last, is bone of my bones
          and flesh of my flesh;
     This one shall be called 'woman,'
          for out of 'her man' this one has been taken."

That is why a man leaves his father and mother
     and clings to his wife,
     and the two of them become one body.

The word of the Lord.

Selection #3

In his love for Rebekah, Isaac found solace after the death of his mother.

A reading from the Book of Genesis   24:48-51, 58-67

The servant of Abraham said to Laban:

"I bowed down in worship to the LORD,
      blessing the LORD, the God of my master Abraham,
      who had led me on the right road
      to obtain the daughter of my master's kinsman for his son.
If, therefore, you have in mind to show true loyalty to my master,
      let me know;
      but if not, let me know that, too.
I can then proceed accordingly."

Laban and his household said in reply:
      "This thing comes from the LORD;
      we can say nothing to you either for or against it.
Here is Rebekah, ready for you;
      take her with you,
      that she may become the wife of your master's son,
      as the LORD has said."

So they called Rebekah and asked her,
      "Do you wish to go with this man?"
She answered, "I do."
At this they allowed their sister Rebekah and her nurse to take leave,
      along with Abraham's servant and his men.
Invoking a blessing on Rebekah, they said:

      "Sister, may you grow
          into thousands of myriads;
      And may your descendants gain possession
          of the gates of their enemies!"

Then Rebekah and her maids started out;
      they mounted their camels and followed the man.
So the servant took Rebekah and went on his way.

Meanwhile Isaac had gone from Beer-lahai-roi
      and was living in the region of the Negeb.
One day toward evening he went out . . . in the field,
      and as he looked around, he noticed that camels were
          approaching.
Rebekah, too, was looking about, and when she saw him,
      she alighted from her camel and asked the servant,
      "Who is the man out there, walking through the fields toward

us?"
"That is my master," replied the servant.
Then she covered herself with her veil.

The servant recounted to Isaac all the things he had done.
Then Isaac took Rebekah into his tent;
     he married her, and thus she became his wife.
In his love for her Isaac found solace
     after the death of his mother Sarah.

The word of the Lord.

Selection #4

May the Lord of heaven prosper you both.
May he grant you mercy and peace.

A reading from the Book of Tobit   7:6-14

Raphael and Tobiah entered the house of Raguel and greeted him.
Raguel sprang up and kissed Tobiah, shedding tears of joy.
But when he heard that Tobit had lost his eyesight,
     he was grieved and wept aloud.
He said to Tobiah:
     "My child, God bless you!
You are the son of a noble and good father.
But what a terrible misfortune
     that such a righteous and charitable man
     should be afflicted with blindness!"
He continued to weep in the arms of his kinsman Tobiah.
His wife Edna also wept for Tobit;
     and even their daughter Sarah began to weep.

Afterward, Raguel slaughtered a ram from the flock
     and gave them a cordial reception.
When they had bathed and reclined to eat,
     Tobiah said to Raphael, "Brother Azariah,
     ask Raguel to let me marry my kinswoman Sarah."
Raguel overheard the words;
     so he said to the boy:
     "Eat and drink and be merry tonight,

for no man is more entitled to marry my daughter Sarah
than you, brother.
Besides, not even I have the right to give her to anyone but you,
because you are my closest relative.
But I will explain the situation to you very frankly.
I have given her in marriage to seven men,
all of whom were kinsmen of ours,
and all died on the very night they approached her.
But now, son, eat and drink.
I am sure the Lord will look after you both."
Tobiah answered, "I will eat or drink nothing
until you set aside what belongs to me."

Raguel said to him: "I will do it.
She is yours according to the decree of the Book of Moses.
Your marriage to her has been decided in heaven!
Take your kinswoman
from now on you are her love,
and she is your beloved.
She is yours today and ever after.
And tonight, son, may the Lord of heaven prosper you both.
May he grant you mercy and peace."
Then Raguel called his daughter Sarah, and she came to him.
He took her by the hand and gave her to Tobiah with the words:
"Take her according to the law.
According to the decree written in the Book of Moses she is your wife.
Take her and bring her back safely to your father.
And may the God of heaven grant both of you peace and prosperity."
He then called her mother and told her to bring a scroll,
so that he might draw up a marriage contract
stating that he gave Sarah to Tobiah as his wife
according to the decree of the Mosaic law.
Her mother brought the scroll,
and he drew up the contract,
to which they affixed their seals.

Afterward they began to eat and drink.

The word of the Lord.

Selection #5

Allow us to live together to a happy old age.

A reading from the Book of Tobit   8:4b-8

On their wedding night Tobiah arose from bed and said to his wife,
    "Sister, get up. Let us pray and beg our Lord
    to have mercy on us and to grant us deliverance."
Sarah got up, and they started to pray
    and beg that deliverance might be theirs.
They began with these words:

    "Blessed are you, O God of our fathers;
        praised be your name forever and ever.
    Let the heavens and all your creation
        praise you forever.
    You made Adam and you gave him his wife Eve
        to be his help and support;
        and from these two the human race descended.
    You said, 'It is not good for the man to be alone;
        let us make him a partner like himself.'
    Now, Lord, you know that I take this wife of mine
        not because of lust,
        but for a noble purpose.
    Call down your mercy on me and on her,
        and allow us to live together to a happy old age."

They said together, "Amen, amen."

The word of the Lord.

Selection #6

The woman who fears the LORD is to be praised.

A reading from the Book of Proverbs   31:10-13, 19-20, 30-31

When one finds a worthy wife,
    her value is far beyond pearls.

Her husband, entrusting his heart to her,
      has an unfailing prize.
She brings him good, and not evil,
      all the days of her life.
She obtains wool and flax
      and makes cloth with skillful hands.
She puts her hands to the distaff,
      and her fingers ply the spindle.
She reaches out her hands to the poor,
      and extends her arms to the needy.
Charm is deceptive and beauty fleeting;
      the woman who fears the LORD is to be praised.
Give her a reward of her labors,
      and let her works praise her at the city gates.

The word of the Lord.

Selection # 7

Stern as death is love.

A reading from the Song of Songs   2:8-10, 14, 16a; 8:6-7a

Hark! my lover–here he comes
      springing across the mountains,
      leaping across the hills.
My lover is like a gazelle
      or a young stag.
Here he stands behind our wall,
      gazing through the windows,
      peering through the lattices.
My lover speaks; he says to me,
      "Arise, my beloved, my dove, my beautiful one, and come!

"O my dove in the clefts of the rock,
      in the secret recesses of the cliff,
Let me see you,
      let me hear your voice,
For your voice is sweet,
      and you are lovely."

My lover belongs to me and I to him.
    He says to me:

"Set me as a seal on your heart,
    as a seal on your arm;
For stern as death is love,
    relentless as the nether-world is devotion;
    its flames are a blazing fire.
Deep waters cannot quench love,
    nor floods sweep it away."

The word of the Lord.

Selection #8

Like the sun rising in the LORD's heavens,
the beauty of a virtuous wife is the radiance of her home.

A reading from the Book of Sirach   26:1-4, 13-16

Blessed the husband of a good wife,
    twice-lengthened are his days;
A worthy wife brings joy to her husband,
    peaceful and full is his life.
A good wife is a generous gift
    bestowed upon him who fears the LORD;
Be he rich or poor, his heart is content,
    and a smile is ever on his face.

A gracious wife delights her husband,
    her thoughtfulness puts flesh on his bones;
A gift from the LORD is her governed speech,
    and her firm virtue is of surpassing worth.
Choicest of blessings is a modest wife
    priceless her chaste soul.
A holy and decent woman adds grace upon grace;
    indeed, no price is worthy of her temperate soul.
Like the sun rising in the LORD's heavens,
    the beauty of a virtuous wife is the radiance of her home.

The word of the Lord.

Selection #9

I will make a new covenant
with the house of Israel and the house of Judah.

A reading from the Book of the Prophet Jeremiah   31:31-32a, 33-34a

The days are coming, says the LORD,
    when I will make a new covenant with the house of Israel
    and the house of Judah.
It will not be like the covenant I made with their fathers:
    the day I took them by the hand
    to lead them forth from the land of Egypt.
But this is the covenant which I will make
    with the house of Israel after those days, says the LORD.
I will place my law within them, and write it upon their hearts;
    I will be their God, and they shall be my people.
No longer will they have need to teach their friends and relatives
    how to know the LORD.
All, from least to greatest, shall know me, says the LORD.

The word of the Lord.

802* READINGS FROM THE NEW TESTAMENT
(choose one)

Selection #1

What will separate us from the love of Christ?

A reading from the Letter of Saint Paul to the Romans   8:31b-35, 37-39

Brothers and sisters:
If God is for us, who can be against us?
He did not spare his own Son
    but handed him over for us all,
      will he not also give us everything else along with him?
Who will bring a charge against God's chosen ones?
It is God who acquits us.
Who will condemn?
It is Christ Jesus who died, rather, was raised,
    who also is at the right hand of God,
    who indeed intercedes for us.
What will separate us from the love of Christ?
Will anguish, or distress, or persecution, or famine,
    or nakedness, or peril, or the sword?

No, in all these things, we conquer overwhelmingly
    through him who loved us.
For I am convinced that neither death, nor life,
    nor angels, nor principalities,
    nor present things, nor future things,
    nor powers, nor height, nor depth,
    nor any other creature will be able to separate us
    from the love of God in Christ Jesus our Lord.

The word of the Lord.

* Number in the Lectionary

LONG FORM

Offer your bodies as a living sacrifice, holy and pleasing to God.

A reading from the Letter of Saint Paul to the Romans   12:1-2, 9-18

I urge you, brothers and sisters, by the mercies of God,
        to offer your bodies as a living sacrifice,
        holy and pleasing to God, your spiritual worship.
Do not conform yourselves to this age
        but be transformed by the renewal of your mind,
        that you may discern what is the will of God,
        what is good and pleasing and perfect.

Let love be sincere;
        hate what is evil,
        hold on to what is good;
        love one another with mutual affection;
        anticipate one another in showing honor.
Do not grow slack in zeal,
        be fervent in spirit,
        serve the Lord.
Rejoice in hope,
        endure in affliction,
        persevere in prayer.
Contribute to the needs of the holy ones,
        exercise hospitality.
Bless those who persecute you,
        bless and do not curse them.
Rejoice with those who rejoice,
        weep with those who weep.
Have the same regard for one another;
        do not be haughty but associate with the lowly;
        do not be wise in your own estimation.
Do not repay anyone evil for evil;
        be concerned for what is noble in the sight of all.
If possible, on your part, live at peace with all.

The word of the Lord.

OR

SHORT FORM

Offer your bodies as a living sacrifice, holy and pleasing to God.

A reading from the Letter of Saint Paul to the Romans   12:1-2, 9-13

I urge you, brothers and sisters, by the mercies of God,
    to offer your bodies as a living sacrifice,
    holy and pleasing to God, your spiritual worship.
Do not conform yourselves to this age
    but be transformed by the renewal of your mind,
    that you may discern what is the will of God
    what is good and pleasing and perfect.

Let love be sincere;
    hate what is evil,
    hold on to what is good;
    love one another with mutual affection;
    anticipate one another in showing honor.
Do not grow slack in zeal,
    be fervent in spirit,
    serve the Lord.
Rejoice in hope,
    endure in affliction,
    persevere in prayer.
Contribute to the needs of the holy ones,
    exercise hospitality.

The word of the Lord.

Selection #3

Welcome one another as Christ welcomed you.

A reading from the Letter of Saint Paul to the Romans 15:1b-3a, 5-7, 13

Brothers and sisters:
We ought to put up with the failings of the weak and not to please
    ourselves;

let each of us please our neighbor for the good,
　　for building up.
For Christ did not please himself.
May the God of endurance and encouragement
　　grant you to think in harmony with one another,
　　in keeping with Christ Jesus,
　　that with one accord you may with one voice
　　glorify the God and Father of our Lord Jesus Christ.

Welcome one another, then, as Christ welcomed you,
　　for the glory of God.
May the God of hope fill you with all joy and peace in believing,
　　so that you may abound in hope by the power of the Holy Spirit.

The word of the Lord.

Selection #4

Your body is a temple of the Spirit.

A reading from the first Letter of Saint Paul to the Corinthians
6:13c-15a, 17-20

Brothers and sisters:
The body is not for immorality, but for the Lord,
　　and the Lord is for the body;
　　God raised the Lord and will also raise us by his power.

Do you not know that your bodies are members of Christ?
Whoever is joined to the Lord becomes one spirit with him.
Avoid immorality.
Every other sin a person commits is outside the body,
　　but the immoral person sins against his own body.
Do you not know that your body
　　is a temple of the Holy Spirit within you,
　　whom you have from God, and that you are not your own?
For you have been purchased at a price.
Therefore glorify God in your body.

The word of the Lord.

If I do not have love, I gain nothing.

**A reading from the first Letter of Saint Paul to the Corinthians
12:31–13:8a**

**Brothers and sisters:
Strive eagerly for the greatest spiritual gifts.**

But I shall show you a still more excellent way.

**If I speak in human and angelic tongues
     but do not have love,
     I am a resounding gong or a clashing cymbal.
And if I have the gift of prophecy
     and comprehend all mysteries and all knowledge;
     if I have all faith so as to move mountains,
     but do not have love, I am nothing.
If I give away everything I own,
     and if I hand my body over so that I may boast
     but do not have love, I gain nothing.**

**Love is patient, love is kind.
It is not jealous, is not pompous,
     it is not inflated, it is not rude,
     it does not seek its own interests,
     it is not quick-tempered, it does not brood over injury, it does
          not rejoice over wrongdoing
     but rejoices with the truth.
It bears all things, believes all things,
     hopes all things, endures all things.
Love never fails.**

The word of the Lord.

Selection #6

This is a great mystery, but I speak in reference to Christ and the Church.

A reading from the Letter of Saint Paul to the Ephesians   5:2a, 21-33

Brothers and sisters:
Live in love, as Christ loved us
      and handed himself over for us.

Be subordinate to one another out of reverence for Christ.
Wives should be subordinate to their husbands as to the Lord.
For the husband is head of his wife
      just as Christ is head of the Church,
      he himself the savior of the body.
As the Church is subordinate to Christ,
      so wives should be subordinate to their husbands in everything.
Husbands, love your wives,
      even as Christ loved the Church
      and handed himself over for her to sanctify her,
      cleansing her by the bath of water with the word,
      that he might present to himself the Church in splendor,
      without spot or wrinkle or any such thing,
      that she might be holy and without blemish.
So also husbands should love their wives as their own bodies.
He who loves his wife loves himself.
For no one hates his own flesh
      but rather nourishes and cherishes it,
      even as Christ does the Church,
      because we are members of his Body.

For this reason a man shall leave his father and his mother
      and be joined to his wife,
and the two shall become one flesh.

This is a great mystery,
      but I speak in reference to Christ and the Church.
In any case, each one of you should love his wife as himself,
      and the wife should respect her husband.

The word of the Lord.

SHORT FORM

This is a great mystery, but I speak in reference to Christ and the Church.

A reading from the Letter of Saint Paul to the Ephesians   5:2a, 25-32

Brothers and sisters:
Live in love, as Christ loved us
        and handed himself over for us.

Husbands, love your wives,
        even as Christ loved the Church
        and handed himself over for her to sanctify her,
        cleansing her by the bath of water with the word,
        that he might present to himself the Church in splendor,
        without spot or wrinkle or any such thing,
        that she might be holy and without blemish.
So also husbands should love their wives as their own bodies.
He who loves his wife loves himself.
For no one hates his own flesh
        but rather nourishes and cherishes it,
        even as Christ does the Church,
        because we are members of his Body.

For this reason a man shall leave his father and his mother
        and be joined to his wife,
and the two shall become one flesh.

This is a great mystery,
        but I speak in reference to Christ and the Church.

The word of the Lord.

Selection #7

The God of peace will be with you.

A reading from the Letter of Saint Paul to the Philippians   4:4-9

Brothers and sisters:
Rejoice in the Lord always.

I shall say it again: rejoice!
Your kindness should be known to all.
The Lord is near.
Have no anxiety at all, but in everything,
       by prayer and petition, with thanksgiving,
       make your requests known to God.
Then the peace of God that surpasses all understanding
       will guard your hearts and minds in Christ Jesus.

Finally, brothers and sisters,
       whatever is true, whatever is honorable,
       whatever is just, whatever is pure,
       whatever is lovely, whatever is gracious,
       if there is any excellence
       and if there is anything worthy of praise,
       think about these things.
Keep on doing what you have learned and received
       and heard and seen in me.
Then the God of peace will be with you.

The word of the Lord.

Selection #8

And over all these put on love,
that is, the bond of perfection.

A reading from the Letter of Saint Paul to the Colossians   3:12-17

Brothers and sisters:
Put on, as God's chosen ones, holy and beloved,
       heartfelt compassion, kindness, humility, gentleness, and
           patience,
       bearing with one another and forgiving one another,
       if one has a grievance against another;
       as the Lord has forgiven you, so must you also do.
And over all these put on love,
       that is, the bond of perfection.
And let the peace of Christ control your hearts,
       the peace into which you were also called in one Body.
And be thankful.

Let the word of Christ dwell in you richly,
   as in all wisdom you teach and admonish one another,
   singing psalms, hymns, and spiritual songs
   with gratitude in your hearts to God.
And whatever you do, in word or in deed,
   do everything in the name of the Lord Jesus,
   giving thanks to God the Father through him.

The word of the Lord.

Selection #9

Let marriage be held in honor by all.

A reading from the Letter to the Hebrews   13:1-4a, 5-6b

Brothers and sisters:
Let mutual love continue.
Do not neglect hospitality,
   for through it some have unknowingly entertained angels.
Be mindful of prisoners as if sharing their imprisonment,
   and of the ill-treated as of yourselves,
   for you also are in the body.
Let marriage be honored among all
   and the marriage bed be kept undefiled.
Let your life be free from love of money
   but be content with what you have,
   for he has said, *I will never forsake you or abandon you.*
Thus we may say with confidence:

   The Lord is my helper,
   and I will not be afraid.

The word of the Lord.

Selection #10

Be of one mind, sympathetic, loving toward one another.

A reading from the first Letter of Saint Peter   3:1-9

Beloved:
You wives should be subordinate to your husbands so that,
      even if some disobey the word,
      they may be won over without a word by their wives' conduct
      when they observe your reverent and chaste behavior.
Your adornment should not be an external one:
      braiding the hair, wearing gold jewelry, or dressing in fine
            clothes,
      but rather the hidden character of the heart,
      expressed in the imperishable beauty
      of a gentle and calm disposition,
      which is precious in the sight of God.
For this is also how the holy women who hoped in God
      once used to adorn themselves
      and were subordinate to their husbands;
      thus Sarah obeyed Abraham, calling him "lord."
You are her children when you do what is good
      and fear no intimidation.

Likewise, you husbands should live with your wives in understanding,
      showing honor to the weaker female sex,
      since we are joint heirs of the gift of life,
      so that your prayers may not be hindered.

Finally, all of you, be of one mind, sympathetic,
      loving toward one another, compassionate, humble.
Do not return evil for evil, or insult for insult;
      but, on the contrary, a blessing, because to this you were called,
      that you might inherit a blessing.

The word of the Lord.

Selection #11

Love in deed and in truth

A reading from the first Letter of Saint John   3:18-24

Children, let us love not in word or speech
      but in deed and truth.

Now this is how we shall know that we belong to the truth
and reassure our hearts before him
in whatever our hearts condemn,
for God is greater than our hearts and knows everything.
Beloved, if our hearts do not condemn us,
we have confidence in God
and receive from him whatever we ask,
because we keep his commandments and do what pleases him.
And his commandment is this:
we should believe in the name of his Son, Jesus Christ,
and love one another just as he commanded us.
Those who keep his commandments remain in him, and he in them,
and the way we know that he remains in us
is from the Spirit that he gave us.

The word of the Lord.

Selection #12

God is love.

A reading from the first Letter of Saint John   4:7-12

Beloved, let us love one another,
because love is of God;
everyone who loves is begotten by God and knows God.
Whoever is without love does not know God, for God is love.
In this way the love of God was revealed to us:
God sent his only-begotten Son into the world
so that we might have life through him.
In this is love:
not that we have loved God, but that he loved us
and sent his Son as expiation for our sins.
Beloved, if God so loved us,
we also must love one another.
No one has ever seen God.
Yet, if we love one another, God remains in us,
and his love is brought to perfection in us.

The word of the Lord.

Blessed are those who have been called to the wedding feast of the Lamb.

A reading from the Book of Revelation   **19:1, 5-9a**

I John, heard what sounded like the loud voice
    of a great multitude in heaven, saying:

      "Alleluia!
Salvation, glory, and might belong to our God."

A voice coming from the throne said:

      "Praise our God, all you his servants,
         and you who revere him, small and great."

Then I heard something like the sound of a great multitude
    or the sound of rushing water or mighty peals of thunder,
    as they said:
      "Alleluia!
The Lord has established his reign,
         our God, the almighty.
Let us rejoice and be glad
         and give him glory.
For the wedding day of the Lamb has come,
         his bride has made herself ready.
She was allowed to wear
         a bright, clean linen garment."
(The linen represents the righteous deeds of the holy ones.)

Then the angel said to me,
    "Write this:
    Blessed are those who have been called
    to the wedding feast of the Lamb."

The word of the Lord.

803* RESPONSORIAL PSALMS
(choose one)

Selection #1

33:12 and 18, 20-21, 22

℟. The earth is full of the goodness of the Lord.

Blessed the nation whose God is the LORD,
    the people he has chosen for his own inheritance.
But see, the eyes of the LORD are upon those who fear him,
    upon those who hope for his kindness.

℟. The earth is full of the goodness of the Lord.

Our soul waits for the LORD,
    who is our help and our shield,
For in him our hearts rejoice;
    in his holy name we trust.

℟. The earth is full of the goodness of the Lord.

May your kindness, O LORD, be upon us
    who have put our hope in you.

℟. The earth is full of the goodness of the Lord.

Selection #2

34:2-3, 4-5, 6-7, 8-9

℟. I will bless the Lord at all times.

or:

℟. Taste and see the goodness of the Lord.

* Number in the Lectionary

112

I will bless the LORD at all times;
    his praise shall be ever in my mouth.
Let my soul glory in the LORD;
    the lowly will hear me and be glad.

℟. I will bless the Lord at all times.

or:

℟. Taste and see the goodness of the Lord.

Glorify the LORD with me,
    let us together extol his name.
I sought the LORD, and he answered me
    and delivered me from all my fears.

℟. I will bless the Lord at all times.

or:

℟. Taste and see the goodness of the Lord.

Look to him that you may be radiant with joy,
    and your faces may not blush with shame.
When the poor one called out, the LORD heard,
    and from all his distress he saved him.

℟. I will bless the Lord at all times.

or:

℟. Taste and see the goodness of the Lord.

The angel of the LORD encamps
    around those who fear him, and delivers them.
Taste and see how good the LORD is;
    blessed the man who takes refuge in him.

℟. I will bless the Lord at all times.

or:

℟. Taste and see the goodness of the Lord.

Selection #3

103:1-2, 8 and 13, 17-18a

℟. The Lord is kind and merciful.

or:

℟. The Lord's kindness is everlasting to those who fear him.

Bless the LORD, O my soul;
and all my being, bless his holy name.
Bless the LORD, O my soul,
and forget not all his benefits.

℟. The Lord is kind and merciful.

or:

℟. The Lord's kindness is everlasting to those who fear him.

Merciful and gracious is the LORD,
slow to anger and abounding in kindness.
As a father has compassion on his children,
so the LORD has compassion on those who fear him.

℟. The Lord is kind and merciful.

or:

℟. The Lord's kindness is everlasting to those who fear him.

But the kindness of the LORD is from eternity
to eternity toward those who fear him,
And his justice towards children's children
among those who keep his covenant.

℟. The Lord is kind and merciful.

or:

℟. The Lord's kindness is everlasting to those who fear him.

Selection # 4

112:1bc-2, 3-4, 5-7a, 7b-8, 9

℟. Blessed the man who greatly delights in the Lord's commands.

or:

℟. Alleluia.

Blessed the man who fears the LORD,
    who greatly delights in his commands.
His posterity shall be mighty upon the earth;
    the upright generation shall be blessed.

℟. Blessed the man who greatly delights in the Lord's commands.

or:

℟. Alleluia.

Wealth and riches shall be in his house;
    his generosity shall endure forever.
Light shines through the darkness for the upright;
    he is gracious and merciful and just.

℟. Blessed the man who greatly delights in the Lord's commands.

or:

℟. Alleluia.

Well for the man who is gracious and lends,
    who conducts his affairs with justice;
He shall never be moved;
    the just one shall be in everlasting remembrance.
An evil report he shall not fear.

℟. Blessed the man who greatly delights in the Lord's commands.

or:

℟. Alleluia.

His heart is firm, trusting in the LORD.
His heart is steadfast; he shall not fear
    till he looks down upon his foes.

        ℟. Blessed the man who greatly delights in the Lord's
        commands.
or:
        ℟. Alleluia.

Lavishly he gives to the poor;
    his generosity shall endure forever;
    his horn shall be exalted in glory.

        ℟. Blessed the man who greatly delights in the Lord's
        commands.
or:
        ℟. Alleluia.

Selection #5

128:1-2, 3, 4-5

        ℟. Blessed are those who fear the Lord.
or:
        ℟. See how the Lord blesses those who fear him.

Blessed are you who fear the LORD,
    who walk in his ways!
For you shall eat the fruit of your handiwork;
    blessed shall you be, and favored.

        ℟. Blessed are those who fear the Lord.
or:
        ℟. See how the Lord blesses those who fear him.

Your wife shall be like a fruitful vine
    in the recesses of your home;
Your children like olive plants
    around your table

℟. Blessed are those who fear the Lord.

or:

℟. See how the Lord blesses those who fear him.

Behold, thus is the man blessed
    who fears the LORD.
The LORD bless you from Zion:
    may you see the prosperity of Jerusalem
    all the days of your life.

℟. Blessed are those who fear the Lord.

or:

℟. See how the Lord blesses those who fear him.

Selection #6

145:8-9, 10 and 15, 17-18

℟. The Lord is compassionate toward all his works.

The LORD is gracious and merciful,
    slow to anger and of great kindness.
The LORD is good to all
    and compassionate toward all his works.

℟. The Lord is compassionate toward all his works.

Let all your works give you thanks, O LORD,
    and let your faithful ones bless you.
The eyes of all look hopefully to you
    and you give them their food in due season.

℟. The Lord is compassionate toward all his works.

The LORD is just in all his ways
    and holy in all his works.
The LORD is near to all who call upon him,
    to all who call upon him in truth.

℟ The Lord is compassionate toward all his works.

Selection #7

148:1-2, 3-4, 9-10, 11-13a, 13c-14a

℟ Let all praise the name of the Lord.

or:

℟ Alleluia.

Alleluia.
Praise the LORD from the heavens,
    praise him in the heights;
Praise him, all you his angels,
    praise him, all you his hosts.

℟ Let all praise the name of the Lord.

or:

℟ Alleluia.

Praise him, sun and moon;
    praise him, all you shining stars.
Praise him, you highest heavens,
    and you waters above the heavens.

℟ Let all praise the name of the Lord.

or:

℟ Alleluia.

You mountains and all you hills,
    you fruit trees and all you cedars;
You wild beasts and all tame animals,
    you creeping things and winged fowl.

℟ Let all praise the name of the Lord.

or:

℟ Alleluia.

Let the kings of the earth and all peoples,
the princes and all the judges of the earth,
Young men too, and maidens,
old men and boys,
Praise the name of the LORD,
for his name alone is exalted.

℟. Let all praise the name of the Lord.
or:
℟. Alleluia.

His majesty is above earth and heaven,
and he has lifted his horn above the people.

℟. Let all praise the name of the Lord.
or:
℟. Alleluia.

804* ALLELUIA VERSES AND VERSES BEFORE THE GOSPEL
(choose one)

1 John 4:7b

Everyone who loves is begotten of God and knows God.

Selection #2

1 John 4:8b, 11

God is love.
If God loved us, we also must love one another.

Selection #3

1 John 4:12

If we love one another,
God remains in us
and his love is brought to perfection in us.

Selection #4

1 John 4:16

Whoever remains in love,
remains in God and God in him.

* Number in the Lectionary

805* READINGS FROM THE GOSPELS
(choose one)

Selection #1

Rejoice and be glad, for your reward will be great in heaven.

+ A reading from the holy Gospel according to Matthew   5:1-12a

When Jesus saw the crowds, he went up the mountain,
   and after he had sat down, his disciples came to him.
He began to teach them, saying:

   "Blessed are the poor in spirit,
      for theirs is the Kingdom of heaven.
   Blessed are they who mourn,
      for they will be comforted.
   Blessed are the meek,
      for they will inherit the land.
   Blessed are they who hunger and thirst for righteousness,
      for they will be satisfied.
   Blessed are the merciful,
      for they will be shown mercy.
   Blessed are the clean of heart,
      for they will see God.
   Blessed are the peacemakers,
      for they will be called children of God.
   Blessed are they who are persecuted for the sake of righteousness,
      for theirs is the Kingdom of heaven.
   Blessed are you when they insult you and persecute you
         and utter every kind of evil against you falsely because of
            me.
   Rejoice and be glad,
      for your reward will be great in heaven."

The Gospel of the Lord.

* Number in the Lectionary

Selection #2

You are the light of the world.

+ A reading from the holy Gospel according to Matthew   5:13-16

Jesus said to his disciples:
"You are the salt of the earth.
But if salt loses its taste, with what can it be seasoned?
It is no longer good for anything
            but to be thrown out and trampled underfoot.
You are the light of the world.
A city set on a mountain cannot be hidden.
Nor do they light a lamp and then put it under a bushel basket;
            it is set on a lamp stand,
            where it gives light to all in the house.
Just so, your light must shine before others,
            that they may see your good deeds
            and glorify your heavenly Father."

The Gospel of the Lord.

Selection #3

LONG FORM

A wise man built his house on rock.

+ A reading from the holy Gospel according to Matthew   7:21, 24-29

Jesus said to his disciples:
"Not everyone who says to me, 'Lord, Lord,'
            will enter the Kingdom of heaven,
            but only the one who does the will of my Father in heaven.

"Everyone who listens to these words of mine and acts on them
            will be like a wise man who built his house on rock.
The rain fell, the floods came,
            and the winds blew and buffeted the house.
But it did not collapse; it had been set solidly on rock.
And everyone who listens to these words of mine
            but does not act on them

will be like a fool who built his house on sand.
The rain fell, the floods came,
      and the winds blew and buffeted the house.
And it collapsed and was completely ruined."

When Jesus finished these words,
      the crowds were astonished at his teaching,
      for he taught them as one having authority,
      and not as their scribes.

The Gospel of the Lord.

OR

SHORT FORM

A wise man built his house on rock.

+ A reading from the holy Gospel according to Matthew   7:21, 24-25

Jesus said to his disciples:
"Not everyone who says to me, 'Lord, Lord,'
      will enter the Kingdom of heaven,
      but only the one who does the will of my Father in heaven.

"Everyone who listens to these words of mine and acts on them
      will be like a wise man who built his house on rock.
The rain fell, the floods came,
      and the winds blew and buffeted the house.
But it did not collapse;
      it had been set solidly on rock."

The Gospel of the Lord.

Selection #4

What God has united, man must not separate.

+ A reading from the holy Gospel according to Matthew   19:3-6

Some Pharisees approached Jesus, and tested him, saying,
      "Is it lawful for a man to divorce his wife for any cause
          whatever?"

He said in reply, "Have you not read that from the beginning
   the Creator *made them male and female* and said,
   For this reason a man shall leave his father and mother
   and be joined to his wife, and the two shall become one flesh?
So they are no longer two, but one flesh.
Therefore, what God has joined together, man must not separate."

The Gospel of the Lord.

Selection #5

This is the greatest and the first commandment.
The second is like it.

+ A reading from the holy Gospel according to Matthew   22:35-40

One of the Pharisees, a scholar of the law, tested Jesus by asking,
   "Teacher, which commandment in the law is the greatest?"
He said to him,
   "You shall love the Lord, your God,
   with all your heart,
   with all your soul,
   and with all your mind.
This is the greatest and the first commandment.
The second is like it:
   You shall love your neighbor as yourself.
The whole law and the prophets depend on these two commandments."

The Gospel of the Lord.

Selection #6

They are no longer two, but one flesh.

+ A reading from the holy Gospel according to Mark   10:6-9

Jesus said:
"From the beginning of creation,
   God made them male and female.
For this reason a man shall leave his father and mother
   and be joined to his wife,
   and the two shall become one flesh.

So they are no longer two but one flesh.
Therefore what God has joined together,
      no human being must separate."

The Gospel of the Lord.

Selection #7

Jesus did this as the beginning of his signs in Cana in Galilee.

✛ A reading from the holy Gospel according to John   2:1-11

There was a wedding in Cana in Galilee,
      and the mother of Jesus was there.
Jesus and his disciples were also invited to the wedding.
When the wine ran short,
      the mother of Jesus said to him,
      "They have no wine."
And Jesus said to her,
      "Woman, how does your concern affect me?
My hour has not yet come."
His mother said to the servers,
      "Do whatever he tells you."
Now there were six stone water jars there for Jewish ceremonial
            washings,
      each holding twenty to thirty gallons.
Jesus told them,
      "Fill the jars with water."
So they filled them to the brim.
Then he told them,
      "Draw some out now and take it to the headwaiter."
So they took it.
And when the headwaiter tasted the water that had become wine,
      without knowing where it came from
      (although the servants who had drawn the water knew),
      the headwaiter called the bridegroom and said to him,
      "Everyone serves good wine first,
      and then when people have drunk freely, an inferior one;
      but you have kept the good wine until now."
Jesus did this as the beginning of his signs in Cana in Galilee
      and so revealed his glory,

and his disciples began to believe in him.

The Gospel of the Lord.

Selection #8

Remain in my love.

+ A reading from the holy Gospel according to John   15:9-12

Jesus said to his disciples:
"As the Father loves me, so I also love you.
Remain in my love.
If you keep my commandments, you will remain in my love,
          just as I have kept my Father's commandments
          and remain in his love.

"I have told you this so that my joy might be in you
          and your joy might be complete.
This is my commandment: love one another as I love you."

The Gospel of the Lord.

Selection #9

This is my commandment: love one another.

+ A reading from the holy Gospel according to John   15:12-16

Jesus said to his disciples:
"This is my commandment: love one another as I love you.
No one has greater love than this,
          to lay down one's life for one's friends.
You are my friends if you do what I command you.
I no longer call you slaves,
          because a slave does not know what his master is doing.
I have called you friends,
          because I have told you everything I have heard from my
                    Father.
It was not you who chose me, but I who chose you
          and appointed you to go and bear fruit that will remain,
          so that whatever you ask the Father in my name he may give
                    you."

The Gospel of the Lord.

Selection #10

That they may be brought to perfection as one.

+ A reading from the holy Gospel according to John   17:20-26

Jesus raised his eyes to heaven and said:
"I pray not only for my disciples,
    but also for those who will believe in me through their word,
    so that they may all be one,
    as you, Father, are in me and I in you,
    that they also may be in us,
    that the world may believe that you sent me.
And I have given them the glory you gave me,
    so that they may be one, as we are one,
    I in them and you in me,
    that they may be brought to perfection as one,
    that the world may know that you sent me,
    and that you loved them even as you loved me.
Father, they are your gift to me.
I wish that where I am they also may be with me,
    that they may see my glory that you gave me,
    because you loved me before the foundation of the world.
Righteous Father, the world also does not know you,
    but I know you, and they know that you sent me.
I made known to them your name and I will make it known,
    that the love with which you loved me
    may be in them and I in them."

The Gospel of the Lord.

OR

That they may be brought to perfection as one.

+ A reading from the holy Gospel according to John   17:20-23

Jesus raised his eyes to heaven and said:

"Holy Father, I pray not only for these,
    but also for those who will believe in me through their word,
    so that they may all be one,
    as you, Father, are in me and I in you,
    that they also may be in us,
    that the world may believe that you sent me.
And I have given them the glory you gave me,
    so that they may be one, as we are one,
    I in them and you in me,
    that they may be brought to perfection as one,
    that the world may know that you sent me,
    and that you loved them even as you loved me."

The Gospel of the Lord.

THE MARRIAGE VOWS

Each answers the questions separately.

Consent To Marriage

The priest invites the couple to declare their consent:

Since it is your intention to enter into marriage, join your right hands, and declare your consent before God and his Church.

The Form Of Consent
They join hands.

Form A *The bridegroom says:*

I, N., take you, N., to be my wife. I promise to be true to you in good times and in bad, in sickness and in health. I will love you and honor you all the days of my life.

The bride says:

I, N., take you, N., to be my husband. I promise to be true to you in good times and in bad, in sickness and in health. I will love you and honor you all the days of my life.

Form B *In dioceses of the United States the following form may be used:*

The bridegroom says:

I, N., take you, N., for my lawful wife, to have and to hold, from this day forward, for better, for worse, for richer, for poorer, in sickness and in health, until death do us part.

The bride says:

I, N., take you, N., for my lawful husband, to have and to hold, from this day forward, for better, for worse, for richer, for poorer, in sickness and in health, until death do us part.

Alternative Forms Of Consent:

Alternative Form A *If, however, it seems preferable for pastoral reasons, the priest may obtain consent from the couple through questions.*

First he asks the bridegroom:

N., do you take N. to be your wife? Do you promise to be true to her in good times and in bad, in sickness and in health, to love her and honor her all the days of your life?
The bridegroom: **I do.**

Then he asks the bride:

N., do you take N. to be your husband? Do you promise to be true to him in good times and in bad, in sickness and in health, to love him and honor him all the days of your life?
The bride: **I do.**

Alternative Form B *In dioceses of the United States the following form may be used:*

First he asks the bridegroom:

N., do you take N. for your lawful wife, to have and to hold, from this day forward, for better, for worse, for richer, for poorer, in sickness and in health, until death do you part?
The bridegroom: **I do.**

Then he asks the bride:

N., do you take N. for your lawful husband, to have and to hold, from this day forward, for better, for worse, for richer, for poorer, in sickness and in health, until death do you part?
The bride: **I do.**

BLESSING AND EXCHANGE OF RINGS

Priest:

A

May the Lord bless ✝ these rings
which you give to each other
as the sign of your love and fidelity.
℟ **Amen**

B

Lord, bless these rings which we bless ✝ in your name.
Grant that those who wear them
may always have a deep faith in each other.
May they do your will
and always live together
in peace, goodwill, and love.
We ask this through Christ our Lord.
℟ **Amen.**

C

Lord,
bless ✝ and consecrate N. and N.
in their love for each other.
May these rings be a symbol
of true faith in each other,
and always remind them of their love.
Through Christ our Lord.
℟ **Amen**

> *The bridegroom places his wife's ring on her ring finger. He may say:*

N., take this ring as a sign of my love and fidelity. In the name of the Father, and of the Son, and of the Holy Spirit.

> *The bride places her husband's ring on his ring finger. She may say:*

N., take this ring as a sign of my love and fidelity. In the name of the Father, and of the Son, and of the Holy Spirit.

GENERAL INTERCESSIONS

PRAYERS OF THE FAITHFUL

Selection A

In confidence, we offer our petitions to God, our Father, through Christ Jesus, our Lord:

𝒱. May ____ and ____ live together in happiness and holiness all the days of their life. We pray to the Lord.

℟. Lord, hear our prayer.

𝒱. May the home and hearts of ____ and ____ be gladdened with children as the fruit of their love. We pray to the Lord.

℟. Lord, hear our prayer.

𝒱. May they be blessed to see their children's children in an atmosphere of peace and joy. We pray to the Lord.

℟. Lord, hear our prayer.

𝒱. May ____ and ____ always walk together in God's Presence and Grace all the days of their life. We pray to the Lord.

℟. Lord, hear our prayer.

𝒱. May Mary, the Mother of God, ever watch over, protect, guide, and guard their family throughout the years. We pray to the Lord.

℟. Lord, hear our prayer.

𝒱. Heavenly Father, may _____ and _____ always walk in Your Light and always do the things that are pleasing in Your sight. May their married life be rich in every kind of good work. We pray to the Lord.

℟. Lord, hear our prayer.

Closing Prayer

Almighty God, our loving Father,
we humbly offer our prayers in Your Presence
for _____ and _____.
Through the Sacred Sacrament of Matrimony
may they grow in happiness and holiness.
May the continuous help of Your Grace abound
in their hearts and in their home; and may
they enjoy the fullness of years together
in marriage.
Grant this through Christ our Lord. Amen.

PRAYERS OF THE FAITHFUL

Selection B

𝒱. May _____ and _____ concern themselves with each other's welfare rather than their own. We pray to the Lord.

℞. Lord, hear our prayer.

𝒱. May their love for one another grow and deepen over the years of their married life. We pray to the Lord.

℞. Lord, hear our prayer.

𝒱. As they mature in years and holiness, may _____ and _____ be the glory of their children; and may their grandchildren be their crown. We pray to the Lord.

℞. Lord, hear our prayer.

𝒱. May _____ and _____ serve Almighty God in righteousness and holiness, as true worshippers, keeping themselves from evildoing, and preserving their innocence. We pray to the Lord.

℞. Lord, hear our prayer.

𝒱. May _____ and _____ always be strong in faith and love, aided by the graces they receive through the Sacrament of Marriage. We pray to the Lord.

℞. Lord, hear our prayer.

𝒱. May God grant _____ and _____ peace; consolation in time of sorrow; health of mind, body, and soul; and at the last, may He grant them eternal happiness in Heaven. We pray to the Lord.

℞. Lord, hear our prayer.

Closing Prayer

Almighty and Loving Father,
we humbly offer these petitions
for our bride and bridegroom.
Today they have vowed before God and
their neighbors to live together in love and fidelity
all the days of their life in the sacred bond of
marriage. With the help of Your Grace,
grant this through Christ our Lord. Amen.

PREFACE FOR MARRIAGE

I

THE DIGNITY OF THE MARRIAGE BOND

Priest: **The Lord be with you.**
People: And also with you.
Priest: **Lift up your hearts.**
People: We lift them up to the Lord.
Priest: **Let us give thanks to the Lord our God.**
People: It is right to give him thanks and praise.

Father, all-powerful and ever-living God,
we do well always and everywhere to give you thanks.

By this sacrament your grace unites man and woman
in an unbreakable bond of love and peace.

You have designed the chaste love of husband and wife
for the increase both of the human family
and of your own family born in baptism.

You are the loving Father of the world of nature;
you are the loving Father of the new creation of grace.
In Christian marriage you bring together the two orders
** of creation:**
nature's gift of children enriches the world
and your grace enriches also your Church.

Through Christ the choir of angels
and all the saints
praise and worship your glory.
May our voices blend with theirs
as we join in their unending hymn:

Holy, holy, holy Lord, God of power and might,
heaven and earth are full of your glory.
**   Hosanna in the highest.**
Blessed is he who comes in the name of the Lord.
**   Hosanna in the highest.**

PREFACE FOR MARRIAGE

II

THE GREAT SACRAMENT OF MARRIAGE

Priest: **The Lord be with you.**
People: And also with you.
Priest: **Lift up your hearts.**
People: We lift them up to the Lord.
Priest: **Let us give thanks to the Lord our God.**
People: It is right to give him thanks and praise.

Father, all-powerful and ever-living God,
we do well always and everywhere to give you thanks
through Jesus Christ our Lord.

Through him you entered into a new covenant with
your people.
You restored man to grace in the saving mystery
of redemption.
You gave him a share in the divine life
through his union with Christ.
You made him an heir of Christ's eternal glory.

This outpouring of love in the new covenant of grace
is symbolized in the marriage covenant
that seals the love of husband and wife
and reflects your divine plan of love.

And so, with the angels and all the saints in heaven
we proclaim your glory
and join in their unending hymn of praise:

Holy, holy, holy Lord, God of power and might,
heaven and earth are full of your glory.
> **Hosanna in the highest.**
Blessed is he who comes in the name of the Lord.
> **Hosanna in the highest.**

PREFACE FOR MARRIAGE

III

MARRIAGE, A SIGN OF GOD'S LOVE

Priest:	**The Lord be with you.**
People:	And also with you.
Priest:	**Lift up your hearts.**
People:	We lift them up to the Lord.
Priest:	**Let us give thanks to the Lord our God.**
People:	It is right to give him thanks and praise.

Father, all-powerful and ever-living God,
we do well always and everywhere to give you thanks.

You created man in love to share your divine life.
We see his high destiny in the love of husband and wife,
which bears the imprint of your own divine love.

Love is man's origin,
love is his constant calling,
love is his fulfillment in heaven.

The love of man and woman
is made holy in the sacrament of marriage,
and becomes the mirror of your everlasting love.

Through Christ the choir of angels
and all the saints
praise and worship your glory.
May our voices blend with theirs
as we join in their unending hymn:

Holy, holy, holy Lord, God of power and might,
heaven and earth are full of your glory.
  Hosanna in the highest.
Blessed is he who comes in the name of the Lord.
  Hosanna in the highest.

AFTERWORD:

Life After The Wedding Cake

My dear friends,

God is responsible for everything that is good in our lives; so God is responsible for marriage and for married life! Marriage is *God's* creation, and by His continuing blessing, marriage is always *sacred* in His sight.

And because *God* is responsible for marriage, every marriage – with no exceptions – must strictly conform to the way in which *God* designed it!

> *...at the beginning the Creator*
> *made them male and female and declared:*
> *That is why a man*
> *leaves his father and mother*
> *and clings to his wife,*
> *and the two of them*
> *become one body.*
> (*Matthew 19:3-4*)
> *"Be fruitful and multiply."*
> (*Genesis 1:28*)

God doesn't ask the impossible of anyone. He gives married persons the *strength* and *ability* to remain faithful to one another in marriage during all the days of their life!

PRAYER OF A HUSBAND AND WIFE FOR EACH OTHER

O Lord Jesus Christ, our Savior and our God,
As husband and wife,
we know that it took three to get married:
the two of us, and You, Lord.
Without You, we know we can do nothing. We humbly
submit ourselves to Your Saving Work in our lives
through the Mass and the Sacraments.
By means of the Grace we receive through the Sacrament
of Matrimony,
Help us to Love You and each other
as perfectly as two humans can love.
Help us to place our faith and trust in You, Lord,
and in each other.
Grant that we may live together with You in grace,
harmony, and peace all the days of our life!
Help us to *support* each other in our weaknesses,
encourage each other with our strengths,
endure each other's faults,
and *forgive* each other's failings.
Grant us the gifts of patience, kindness, gentleness,
and cheerfulness;
and a spirit of loving concern for the well-being
of each other, ahead of ourself.
Grant that the love which brought us together in marriage,
will mature and grow day-by-day.
Let our love for each other bring us ever closer to You, our Loving God.
And if it be Your Will, O Lord, please grant us children
as the fruit of our love.
Amen.

Would you like more copies of

"LOVE, DATING, AND MARRIAGE"?

This book is a treasure for those who plan to marry some day;
those who are already married;
and those who are about to marry in the near future.

is an easy to use, practical guide for:

- Instruction in preparation for Marriage

- Preparing a Wedding Ceremony

- Parents whose children are approaching adolescence

- Teenage Confirmation instruction

- Theological reflection on Married life

- Answering questions about True Love

- Learning the "why", "what-for", and "how" of Dating

- Appreciating the challenges and blessings of Marriage

Order by calling Leaflet Missal Company toll free 1-888-532-3538

AND

Have you read Fr. Papa's Book entitled:

"TEENAGE GUIDE FOR CONFESSION"?

- Already in its Second Printing, 50,000 copies sold!

- Easy to carry in pocket or purse!

- Addressed to Teens, but popular with young people and adults alike!

- Handy, helpful guide for making an Examination of Conscience.

Order by calling Leaflet Missal Company toll free 1-888-532-3538

□ Alleluia Verse and Verse Before the Gospel: #_____,
page _____

□ Gospel Reading: #_____, page _____
For Selection #3 or #10 please indicate: □ Long Form
□ Short Form

The Marriage Vows

□ Form "A", page 129

□ Form "B", page 129

□ *Alternative* Form "A", page 130

□ *Alternative* Form "B", page 130

The Blessing And Exchange Of Rings

□ Blessing "A", page 131

□ Blessing "B", page 131

□ Blessing "C", page 131

Prayers Of The Faithful

□ Prayers Of The Faithful "A", page 132

□ Prayers Of The Faithful "B", page 133

Preface Prayers For Marriage

□ Preface Selection I, page 134

□ Preface Selection II, page 135

□ Preface Selection III, page 136

The Wedding Mass

PULL-OUT FORM

To indicate your preferences for:

Choice of Wedding Mass Prayers; Wedding Readings; Form of Consent to Marriage; Blessing of Rings; Prayers of the Faithful; Preface Prayers. ("Wedding Preparation Checklist" is included).

The Wedding Mass Prayers

☐ Wedding Mass Prayers Set **A** ___ **B** ___ **C** ___ page ____

Or The Wedding Mass Prayers May Be Interchanged:

☐ *Opening Prayer* From Set **A** ___ **B** ___ **C** ___ page ____

☐ *Prayer Over Gifts* From Set **A** ___ **B** ___ **C** ___ page ____

☐ *Prayer After Communion* From Set **A** ___ **B** ___ **C** ___ page ____

The Wedding Mass Readings

☐ Old Testament Reading: #_____, page _____

☐ New Testament Reading: #_____, page _____
    For Selection #2 or #6 please indicate: ☐ Long Form
                                            ☐ Short Form

☐ Responsorial Psalm: #_____, page _____